Parallel Python with Dask

Perform distributed computing, concurrent programming and manage large dataset

Tim Peters

Copyright © 2023 by GitforGits

All rights reserved. This book is protected under copyright laws and no part of it may be reproduced or transmitted in any form or by any means, electronic or mechanical, including photocopying, recording, or by any information storage and retrieval system, without the prior written permission of the publisher. Any unauthorized reproduction, distribution, or transmission of this work may result in civil and criminal penalties and will be dealt with in the respective jurisdiction at anywhere in India, in accordance with the applicable copyright laws.

Published by: GitforGits
Publisher: Sonal Dhandre
www.gitforgits.com
support@gitforgits.com

Printed in India

First Printing: October 2023

ISBN: 978-8119177653

Cover Design by: Kitten Publishing

For permission to use material from this book, please contact GitforGits at support@gitforgits.com.

Prologue

The advent of big data and the exponential growth in the complexity of computational tasks have necessitated a paradigm shift in the way we approach programming and data processing. Traditional sequential processing methods are no longer sufficient to handle the vast amounts of data and the intricate algorithms that modern applications require. Parallel computing has emerged as a vital solution to these challenges, enabling the simultaneous execution of computations and thereby significantly reducing processing time.

"Parallel Python with Dask" is a comprehensive guide that takes you on a journey through the world of parallel computing using Python's Dask library. Dask is a flexible parallel computing library that integrates seamlessly with the existing Python ecosystem. It allows you to harness the power of parallelism without having to delve into the low-level intricacies of parallel programming.

The book is structured into ten chapters, each focusing on a specific aspect of parallel computing and Dask. Starting with an introduction to parallel processing and the limitations of traditional computing methods, the book gradually builds up to more advanced topics such as distributed systems, GPU computing, and integration with various machine learning frameworks like Scikit-Learn and PyTorch.

Chapter one lays the foundation by introducing the concept of CPU computing and the transition to GPU computing. Subsequent chapters delve into Dask's architecture, its collections, computational models, and how it interfaces with popular data processing libraries like Pandas and NumPy. The book also explores the integration of Dask with machine learning libraries, providing practical examples and insights into optimizing models for parallel execution.

A unique feature of this book is its hands-on approach. Each chapter is filled with practical examples, sample programs, and step-by-step instructions that allow you to apply the concepts you learn in real-world scenarios. Whether you are dealing with dataframes, arrays, or machine learning models, the book provides you with the tools and knowledge to parallelize your tasks efficiently. Moreover, the book doesn't just stop at teaching you how to use Dask. It goes beyond that by learning best practices, optimization strategies, and techniques for managing resources in distributed systems. It also covers advanced topics like fault tolerance and scaling, essential for building robust and scalable parallel applications.

"Parallel Python with Dask" is not just a book for Python developers or data scientists. It's a resource for anyone who wants to unlock the potential of parallel computing, whether you are a student, researcher, or professional. The book assumes a basic understanding of Python and familiarity with data processing but does not require prior knowledge of parallel computing.

By the end of this book, you will have a thorough understanding of parallel computing principles and how to implement them using Dask. You will be equipped with the skills to write efficient, scalable code that can handle large datasets and complex computations. More importantly, you will have the confidence to apply these skills in your projects, transforming the way you approach programming and data processing.

In a world where data is growing at an unprecedented rate, the ability to process it quickly and efficiently is paramount. "Parallel Python with Dask" is your guide to mastering parallel computing, enabling you to take on the challenges of modern data processing with confidence and skill. Whether you aspire to become a proficient Python developer or a skilled machine learning engineer, this book will be an invaluable asset in your journey towards achieving those goals.

Content

Prologue iii
Preface ix
CHAPTER 1: INTRODUCTION TO DASK 1
   Need for Parallel Computing 2
   Lazy Evaluation? 3
      Overview 3
      Benefits 4
   Destination to Dask 4
      Dask vs PySpark 5
      Dask vs Airflow 6
      Dask vs Celery 6
   Dask Applications & Use-cases 7
      Large-Scale Data Analysis 7
      Machine Learning 7
      Image Processing 7
   Prepare Linux for Dask 8
      Getting Linux Ready! 8
      Installing Dask with pip 9
      Installing Dask with conda 9
   Dask Architecture 10
      Architecture Overview 10
      Architecture Mechanism 10
   Task Scheduling in Dask 11
      Node, Task & Scheduler 11
      Threaded Scheduler 12
      Processes Scheduler 12
      Distributed Scheduler 12
   Dask Collection 13

- Dask Arrays 13
- Dask DataFrames 13
- Dask Bags 13
- Dask Delayed 14
- **Computational Model in Dask** 14
  - Task Graphs 14
  - Lazy Evaluation 14
  - Schedulers 14
  - Parallel and Distributed Computing 15
  - Integration with Python Scientific Stack 15
- **Summary** 15

CHAPTER 2: DASK FUNDAMENTALS 17

- **Overview** 18
- **Dask Arrays** 19
  - Creating a Dask Array 20
  - Loading Data into Dask Array 21
  - Performing Operations on Dask Array 21
  - Storing Dask Array 22
- **Dask Dataframes** 22
  - Creating Dask DataFrame 24
  - Loading Data into Dask DataFrame 25
  - Performing Operations on Dask DataFrame 25
  - Storing Dask DataFrame 25
- **Dask Bags** 26
  - Key Features 26
- **Performing Dask Bag Operations** 27
  - Creating Dask Bag 28
  - Loading Data into Dask Bag 28
  - Performing Operations on Dask Bag 28
  - Storing Dask Bag 28
- **Dask Delayed** 29

    Applying Dask Delayed 29

Dask Futures 31

    Applying Dask Futures 31

Dask Dashboard 33

Performance Profiling in Dask 37

Dask's Memory Management 38

    Sample Program: Automate Management of Memory 39

Error Handling in Dask 40

    Sample Program: Handling Errors 41

Summary 44

CHAPTER 3: BATCH DATA PARALLEL PROCESSING WITH DASK **45**

    Introduction to Batch Processing 46

    Parallel Processing Concepts 46

    Parallel Batch Processing Procedure 48

    Sample Program: Perform Batch Processing 49

    Applying Dask on Large Dataset 51

    Introduction to Dask Partitioning 53

    Determining Partitions 54

    Task Graphs 55

    Summary 56

CHAPTER 4: DISTRIBUTED SYSTEMS AND DASK **58**

    Distributed Systems Overview 59

    Understanding Distributed Scheduler in Dask 60

    Configure Distributed Cluster 62

    Monitor Dask Clusters 63

    Distributed Task Scheduling 65

    Optimization Strategies for Task Scheduling 66

    Implement Work Stealing 67

    Run Prefetching 68

    Instrument Data Locality 69

    Implement Dynamic Scheduling 70

Deploy Task Fusion 72

Understanding Fault Tolerance 73

Scaling Dask Clusters 74

Resource Usage and Management 76

Summary 77

CHAPTER 5: ADVANCED DASK: APIS AND BUILDING BLOCKS 78

Introduction to Algorithms 79

Custom Algorithms? 79

Exploring Dask Joblib 81

Parallelizing Code using Joblib 82

Understanding Numba 84

Integrate Dask with Numba 85

   Define Function with Numba 85

   Create Dask Arrays 86

   Apply Function to Dask Arrays 86

   Compute the Result 86

Understanding NumPy 87

Integrate Dask with NumPy 88

   Import Dask and NumPy 88

   Create Large NumPy Array 88

   Convert NumPy Array to Dask Array 88

   Perform Operations on Dask Array 88

   Compute Result 89

Exploring Xarray 89

Integrate Dask with Xarray 90

   Import Dask, Xarray, and NumPy 90

   Create Large Dask Array 91

   Convert Dask Array to Xarray DataArray 91

   Perform Operations on Xarray DataArray 91

   Compute Result 91

Summary 92

CHAPTER 6: INTEGRATED LIBRARIES: DASK WITH PANDAS 93

- Pandas Overview 94
- Creating Dask DataFrame 94
- Group Operations with Dask and Pandas 96
- Executing Joint Operations 97
- Performing Time-series Analysis 98
- Performance Analysis of Dask and Pandas 99
- Summary 100

CHAPTER 7: INTEGRATED LIBRARIES: DASK WITH SCIKIT-LEARN 101

- Scikit-learn Overview 102
- Parallelizing Scikit-learn Models 103
- Performing Model Selection 105
- Running Model Evaluation 107
- Hyperparameter Tuning 109
- Preprocessing and Feature Extraction 111
- Understanding Large-scale Machine Learning 112
- Scikit-learn Best Practices 114
- Summary 116

CHAPTER 8: INTEGRATED LIBRARIES: DASK AND PYTORCH 118

- PyTorch Overview 119
- Using PyTorch with Dask 120
- Parallelizing Deep Learning Operations 123
- Running PyTorch Model in Parallel 124
- Distributed Training of PyTorch Model 126
- Model Evaluation and Hyperparameter Tuning 128
  - Model Evaluation 128
  - Hyperparameter Tuning 129
- PyTorch Best Practices 130
- Summary 132

CHAPTER 9: DASK WITH GPUS 133

- Understanding GPU Computing 134

Dask for GPU Computing 135
Performing GPU Computing with Dask 136
What is RAPIDS? 138
    Core Components 138
    Dask's Integration with RAPIDS 138
What is Google JAX? 140
    Core Features 140
    Dask's Integration with Google JAX 140
Summary 141

CHAPTER 10: SCALING MACHINE LEARNING PROJECTS WITH DASK 143

Structure of Machine Learning Projects 144
Introduction to DaskML 145
    Purpose of DaskML 146
    How DaskML Functions 146
Machine Learning Workloads with DaskML 147
    Managing Machine Learning Workloads with DaskML 147
Managing Regression Model using DaskML 148
Managing Classification Model 150
DaskML Key Functions 151
Summary 152
Index 154
Epilogue 156

Preface

"Parallel Python with Dask" is a comprehensive guide designed to empower aspiring Python professionals and machine learning engineers with the skills to harness the power of parallel computing. Through a meticulously crafted journey across ten chapters, this book explores the world of Dask, a flexible parallel computing library that integrates seamlessly with the Python ecosystem.

The book begins with an introduction to parallel and batch processing, laying the foundation for understanding how Dask can optimize computational tasks. It then delves into the intricacies of parallel processing, task scheduling, and data partitioning, providing practical examples and step-by-step guidance. As you progress, they will explore the integration of Dask with various libraries and frameworks such as Pandas, Scikit-Learn, PyTorch, Numba, Numpy, and Xarray. Each chapter builds on the previous one, offering insights into handling different machine learning workloads, from regression and classification models to hyperparameter tuning and feature extraction.

The chapters on GPU computing and Dask's integration with RAPIDS and Google JAX offer a deep dive into the cutting-edge technology of GPU-accelerated computing. Readers will learn how to leverage the GPU's parallel processing capabilities to achieve remarkable performance gains. A special focus is given to scalability, with chapters dedicated to distributed systems, cluster management, resource utilization, and best practices for using Dask with various machine learning frameworks. Real-world examples and case studies provide a hands-on approach, enabling you to apply the concepts learned to their own projects.

The final chapters of the book explore DaskML, a specialized library for managing machine learning workloads, and the integration of Dask with popular deep learning frameworks. These chapters equip you with the knowledge to scale their machine learning models efficiently and effectively.

In this book you will learn how to:

- Comprehensive understanding of parallel computing, enhancing efficiency in data processing and machine learning tasks.
- In-depth exploration of Dask's architecture, enabling optimized task scheduling and data partitioning.
- Integration techniques with Pandas, Scikit-Learn, and PyTorch, expanding parallel processing capabilities.
- Practical guidance on GPU computing, unlocking the potential of GPU-accelerated performance.

- Hands-on examples of managing ML workloads, providing real-world applicability.
- Insights into scalability and distributed systems, essential for handling large-scale data.
- Techniques for resource utilization and management, ensuring optimal performance in distributed environments.
- Exploration of DaskML for managing regression and classification models, tailored for machine learning.
- Best practices for using Dask with various frameworks, ensuring effective parallelization strategies.

To ensure you get the most out of this book, each chapter includes hands-on examples and exercises to reinforce your understanding of the concepts presented. You'll also learn to optimize your Rust code and select the best tools and libraries for each task, maximizing your productivity and efficiency.

GitforGits

Prerequisites

In a world where data is at the core of decision-making, innovation, and progress, the ability to process it efficiently is a valuable asset. Whether you are a developer, data scientist, researcher, or enthusiast, the knowledge gained from this book empowers you to contribute to this exciting field and in your profession too.

Codes Usage

Are you in need of some helpful code examples to assist you in your programming and documentation? Look no further! Our book offers a wealth of supplemental material, including code examples and exercises.

Not only is this book here to aid you in getting your job done, but you have our permission to use the example code in your programs and documentation. However, please note that if you are reproducing a significant portion of the code, we do require you to contact us for permission.

But don't worry, using several chunks of code from this book in your program or answering a question by citing our book and quoting example code does not require permission. But if you do choose to give credit, an attribution typically includes the title, author, publisher, and ISBN. For example, "Parallel Python with Dask by Tim Peters".

If you are unsure whether your intended use of the code examples falls under fair use or the permissions outlined above, please do not hesitate to reach out to us at support@gitforgits.com.

We are happy to assist and clarify any concerns.

Acknowledgement

I owe a tremendous debt of gratitude to GitforGits, for their unflagging enthusiasm and wise counsel throughout the entire process of writing this book. Their knowledge and careful editing helped make sure the piece was useful for people of all reading levels and comprehension skills. In addition, I'd like to thank everyone involved in the publishing process for their efforts in making this book a reality. Their efforts, from copyediting to advertising, made the project what it is today.

Finally, I'd like to express my gratitude to everyone who has shown me unconditional love and encouragement throughout my life. Their support was crucial to the completion of this book. I appreciate your help with this endeavour and your continued interest in my career.

Chapter 1: Introduction to Dask

Need for Parallel Computing

In the world of computing, there is a never-ending search for faster and more efficient methods. The need for faster data processing and analysis is becoming more pressing as the volume of data continues to increase at an exponential rate. The use of parallel computing becomes necessary at this point. One type of computing is known as parallel computing, and it is characterized by the execution of multiple calculations or processes in parallel with one another. It is predicated on the idea that large problems can frequently be broken down into a series of smaller problems, which can then be solved simultaneously, also known as "in parallel." This strategy can cut the amount of time required for computation by a significant amount, which is especially helpful when dealing with complex computational tasks or large-scale data analyses.

A number of different considerations have led to the requirement for parallel computing. The sheer amount of data that is being generated in today's world is the first and most important factor to consider. The advent of the digital age has resulted in a data production rate that is unprecedented. This information originates from a wide variety of sources, including social media, devices connected to the internet of things (IoT), scientific experiments, business transactions, and more. The processing and analysis of this data using conventional sequential computing methods is not only labor- and time-intensive, but it also requires a significant amount of computational power. Computing in parallel offers a solution to this issue by breaking the data down into smaller pieces that can then be processed simultaneously, which cuts down significantly on the total amount of time required for the processing.

The growing complexity of computational problems is another factor that is driving the need for parallel computing. The computational tasks involved in fields such as artificial intelligence, bioinformatics, climate modeling, and quantum physics are so complex that they cannot be efficiently solved by sequential computing. By dividing these tasks up into smaller, more manageable tasks that can be solved concurrently, parallel computing paves the way for the solution of complex problems that would otherwise be computationally impossible to solve.

The development of computers with multiple cores and processors has also added fuel to the fire that is the demand for parallel computing. Computers built in the last few decades typically have multiple cores or processors, each of which is capable of carrying out tasks independently of the others. However, in order to get the most out of these hardware capabilities, the software needs to be designed so that it can carry out tasks simultaneously. Computing in parallel is the solution to this problem. We are able to fully utilize the capabilities of modern hardware and achieve significant improvements in performance by designing algorithms and software that are capable of executing tasks in parallel. In addition to this, the proliferation of distributed computing systems, such as cloud computing platforms, has further amplified the demand for parallel computing. These systems are made up of a number of computers or servers that collaborate with one another to carry out computations. Typically, these computers or servers are located in a variety of physical locations. It is necessary to partition tasks and carry them out in parallel across a number of computers or servers if one wishes to make efficient use of distributed resources.

The demand for parallel computing is especially pronounced when considering Python, which is recognized as one of the most widely used high-level programming languages. Python is a widely used programming language that finds applications in a variety of fields, including data analysis, machine learning, web development, and many others. Nevertheless, the default execution model for Python is sequential, which means that it only works through one operation at a time. When working with large datasets or performing complex computations, this can be a significant bottleneck in the process. Dask, a Python library that allows for flexible parallel computing, provides a solution to this problem. It makes it possible to take Python code that already exists and easily scale it up so that it can handle larger datasets or more complex computations. You will be able to take advantage of the power of parallel computing with Dask, without having to make significant changes to the Python code you are already using.

Lazy Evaluation?

Overview

Lazy evaluation, also known as call-by-need, is a strategy in programming where the evaluation of expressions is delayed until their results are actually needed. This is in contrast to eager evaluation, the more common strategy where expressions are evaluated as soon as they are encountered. The concept of lazy evaluation is not new and has been a fundamental aspect of certain programming languages, particularly functional languages like Haskell. However, it has gained more attention in recent years due to its applicability in handling large datasets and improving computational efficiency, especially in the realm of parallel and distributed computing.

The primary advantage of lazy evaluation is that it can potentially save significant amounts of computational resources. By delaying computation until it's absolutely necessary, we avoid performing unnecessary calculations. This can be particularly beneficial when dealing with large datasets or complex computations. For instance, if we have a large dataset and we're interested in a small subset that satisfies a certain condition, with lazy evaluation, we can avoid loading the entire dataset into memory and only compute the values for the subset we're interested in.

Lazy evaluation also enables us to work with infinite data structures or streams of data. Since computations are only performed when needed, we can define infinite data structures without running into memory issues. This is particularly useful in scenarios such as streaming data processing, where data is continuously generated and we're interested in performing computations on the fly. In the context of parallel computing, lazy evaluation can help optimize the execution of tasks. Since the actual computation is delayed until necessary, a system can schedule tasks more efficiently based on the current workload and resource availability. This can lead to better utilization of computational resources and improved performance.

We shall learn how lazy evaluation works in Dask. Dask uses lazy evaluation extensively in its computations. When you perform operations using Dask, it doesn't immediately execute them. Instead, it records these operations in a task graph, which is a visual representation of the computation that outlines the dependencies between tasks. The actual computation is not carried out until you explicitly ask Dask to compute the result, a process known as 'materializing' the computation.

Benefits

This approach has several benefits as below:

- First, it allows Dask to perform various optimizations on the task graph before executing the computation. These optimizations can include rearranging or merging tasks to reduce the overall computation time, minimizing memory usage, or balancing the workload across different cores or nodes in a cluster.

- Second, by building a task graph, Dask can parallelize the computation effectively. Tasks that are independent of each other can be run in parallel, allowing for efficient use of multicore processors or distributed computing resources.

- Third, the task graph provides a clear visualization of the computation, which can be useful for debugging or understanding the computation process. Dask provides tools to visualize the task graph, allowing you to see the sequence of operations and their dependencies.

The ability to delay computation until necessary, optimize task execution, and parallelize tasks effectively is invaluable. Lazy evaluation is a powerful tool in Dask's arsenal, enabling it to handle large, complex computations in an efficient manner. However, it's important to remember that while lazy evaluation has many benefits, it's not always the best strategy. There are cases where eager evaluation might be more appropriate. For instance, if the result of a computation is needed immediately, or if the computation is simple and quick, eager evaluation might be more efficient.

Destination to Dask

Building on the concepts of parallel computing and lazy evaluation, we shall now explore the purpose behind the creation of Dask. Dask was developed to fill a specific need in the Python data science ecosystem, and understanding this purpose can provide valuable insight into how and why Dask is used today.

Python has long been a popular language for data analysis due to its readability, flexibility, and the strength of its scientific computing libraries like NumPy, Pandas, and Scikit-Learn. However, these libraries were primarily designed to work with in-memory data that fits comfortably on a single machine. As data sizes grew beyond the memory capacity of a single machine, Python's data science ecosystem faced a scalability problem. The traditional solution to this problem was to move to a distributed computing framework like Apache Hadoop or Spark. However, these frameworks require users to write code in a specific style or even in a different language (like Java or Scala), and they don't integrate well with Python's existing scientific computing libraries. This created a gap for users who wanted to scale their computations without leaving the comfort of the Python ecosystem or rewriting their existing code.

Dask was developed to fill this gap. Its primary purpose is to enable scalable computations on large datasets, while integrating seamlessly with Python's existing data science stack. Dask achieves this by providing parallel, larger-than-memory computations that can be distributed across multiple machines. Moreover, Dask's API is designed to mimic the APIs of popular Python libraries like NumPy and Pandas, making it easy for Python users to scale their existing workflows. Another key purpose of Dask is to provide a flexible and adaptable tool for parallel computing. While other parallel computing libraries often require users to fit their problems into a specific computational model (like MapReduce), Dask is designed to be more flexible. It provides low-level primitives for building custom parallel computing systems, as well as high-level interfaces for common computational patterns. This makes Dask suitable for a wide range of tasks, from simple parallel computations to complex machine learning workflows.

Dask also aims to improve the performance of Python's scientific computing stack. By using lazy evaluation and building task graphs, Dask can optimize computations and make efficient use of computational resources. This can lead to significant performance improvements, especially for large-scale computations. Furthermore, Dask is designed to be a community-driven project. Its developers aim to create a tool that is not only powerful and flexible, but also accessible and easy to use. They actively encourage contributions from the community and strive to create a welcoming and inclusive environment for users and contributors alike.

Now it is also important to understand how Dask differentiates itself from other parallel computing tools in the Python ecosystem. We shall now compare Dask with some of its direct competitors such as PySpark, Airflow, and Celery.

Dask vs PySpark

PySpark is the Python API for Apache Spark, a popular distributed computing system. Both Dask and PySpark provide distributed data processing capabilities, but there are several key differences between them.

1. Firstly, Dask is fully implemented in Python and integrates seamlessly with the Python ecosystem. It's designed to work well with familiar Python libraries like NumPy, Pandas, and Scikit-Learn. On the other hand, Spark is written in Scala and its primary interface is the Scala API. PySpark provides a Python interface to Spark, but it's not as seamless or as

performant as the Scala API.

2. Secondly, Dask's API is more flexible and Pythonic. It provides both low-level primitives for complex and custom parallelism, and high-level interfaces that mimic NumPy and Pandas. PySpark, on the other hand, requires users to work with Spark's specific data structures (like RDDs and DataFrames) and computational models.

3. Finally, Dask is generally lighter-weight and easier to install and use on a single machine, while Spark is designed for large-scale, distributed computations and can be more complex to set up and configure.

Dask vs Airflow

1. Airflow is a platform to programmatically author, schedule, and monitor workflows. While Dask is a library for parallel computing, Airflow is more of a workflow management system.

2. Airflow is designed to manage complex workflows that involve dependencies between tasks. It provides a rich set of features for scheduling, monitoring, and managing workflows, and it's particularly well-suited for ETL (Extract, Transform, Load) tasks and data pipelines.

3. On the other hand, Dask is designed for parallel and distributed computing. It's more focused on executing computations efficiently, rather than managing workflows. Dask doesn't have built-in support for scheduling or monitoring workflows like Airflow does.

In other words, Dask and Airflow serve different purposes and are often used together. You might use Airflow to manage and schedule your workflows, and use Dask to perform the actual computations within those workflows.

Dask vs Celery

Celery is an asynchronous task queue/job queue based on distributed message passing. It's focused on real-time operation, but supports scheduling as well. Celery is a great tool for background tasks, especially for web applications where you need to perform tasks outside the usual request-response cycle. It's also good for simple distributed computing tasks, where you need to distribute tasks across multiple workers.

Dask, on the other hand, is more suited for complex, large-scale computations. It provides more advanced features for parallel computing, like task dependencies and lazy evaluation. Dask also integrates well with the Python scientific stack, which makes it a good choice for data-intensive computations.

Dask, PySpark, Airflow, and Celery, they all provide capabilities for distributed computing, they each have their own strengths and are suited to different types of tasks. Dask's strength lies in its seamless integration with the Python ecosystem, its flexible and Pythonic API, and its capabilities for large-scale, data-intensive computations.

Dask Applications & Use-cases

Large-Scale Data Analysis

One of the most common use-cases for Dask is in large-scale data analysis. Dask's data structures extend common interfaces like NumPy arrays and Pandas DataFrames to larger-than-memory and distributed environments. These allow users to scale their existing workflows with minimal code changes.

For instance, consider a scenario where a data scientist needs to analyze a large dataset of web traffic logs to understand user behavior. The dataset is several terabytes in size, far too large to fit into memory on a single machine. With Dask, the data scientist can read the data into a Dask DataFrame, which is a large parallel DataFrame composed of many smaller Pandas DataFrames split along the index. Dask DataFrames mimic the Pandas API, so the data scientist can use familiar Pandas operations like groupby, join, and time-series aggregation.

Machine Learning

Dask is also commonly used in machine learning workflows, particularly for training models on large datasets. Dask-ML is a Python library for scalable machine learning in Python which is built on top of Dask.

Consider a scenario where a data scientist is working on a machine learning model to predict customer churn. The dataset is large and high-dimensional, making it computationally expensive to train a model using Scikit-Learn on a single machine. With Dask-ML, the data scientist can train the model on a cluster of machines. Dask-ML provides scalable machine learning algorithms that integrate well with Dask arrays and DataFrames. It includes implementations of popular algorithms like linear models, clustering, and preprocessing methods that can scale to large datasets. Moreover, Dask-ML provides utilities for model selection (like GridSearchCV and RandomizedSearchCV) that can be parallelized across a Dask cluster. This allows the data scientist to tune hyperparameters more quickly and efficiently.

Image Processing

Dask is also used in image processing tasks, particularly for processing large images or collections of images. Dask arrays, which extend NumPy arrays to larger-than-memory and distributed environments, are particularly well-suited for this task.

For example, consider a scenario where a researcher is working with a large set of high-resolution satellite images. The researcher wants to apply a complex image processing algorithm to each image, but the size of the images makes this computationally expensive. With Dask, the researcher can represent the collection of images as a large Dask array. The image processing algorithm can be implemented as a function that operates on NumPy arrays, and then applied to the Dask array using the map_blocks or map_overlap methods. Dask takes care of scheduling the computations and executing them in parallel, allowing the researcher to process the images more quickly and efficiently.

Dask is a versatile tool that can be used in a wide range of scenarios. Its ability to scale computations with minimal code changes, combined with its integration with the Python scientific stack, makes it a powerful tool for large-scale data analysis, machine learning, and image processing.

Prepare Linux for Dask

To use Dask for your data processing needs, you first need to install it on your system. The installation process involves preparing your Linux environment and then installing Dask using package managers like pip or conda. We shall now walk through these steps in detail.

Getting Linux Ready!

Before you can install Dask, you need to confirm that your Linux environment is set up with the necessary prerequisites. The primary requirement is Python. Dask is a Python library, and it requires Python 3.5 or later. Most modern Linux distributions come with Python pre-installed, but you can check your Python version by opening a terminal and typing:

```
python --version
```

If you don't have Python installed, or if your Python version is older than 3.5, you'll need to install a newer version of Python. On Ubuntu, you can do this with the following commands:

```
sudo apt update
sudo apt install python3.11.5
```

Replace "3.11.5" with the version of Python you wish to install, incase you wish to use a specific version.

You'll also need a package manager to install Dask. The two most common package managers for

Python are pip and conda. pip is included by default with Python 3.4 and later, so if you have a suitable version of Python installed, you should already have pip. You can check your pip version with:

```
pip --version
```

If you don't have pip installed, you can install it on Ubuntu with:

```
sudo apt install python3-pip
```

conda is a package manager that comes with the Anaconda distribution of Python. If you plan to use conda to install Dask, you'll need to install Anaconda. You can download Anaconda from the official website and follow the installation instructions provided there.

Installing Dask with pip

Once your environment is prepared, you can install Dask using pip. To do this, open a terminal and type:

```
pip install "dask[complete]"
```

This command installs Dask along with all optional dependencies. These optional dependencies provide additional functionality, but are not necessary for a basic installation of Dask.

Installing Dask with conda

Alternatively, you can install Dask using conda. This can be particularly useful if you're using the Anaconda distribution of Python, which is popular for data science work. To install Dask with conda, open a terminal and type:

```
conda install -c conda-forge dask
```

This command installs Dask from the conda-forge channel, which is a community-led collection of packages for conda. After Dask is installed, you can verify the installation by opening a Python interpreter and importing Dask:

```
import dask
```

If Dask is installed correctly, this command should not produce any errors.

Dask Architecture

Having successfully installed Dask, gaining a deep understanding of its architectural framework is essential for effectively leveraging its extensive capabilities. Dask's architecture is meticulously designed to facilitate both parallel and distributed computing. This design enables users to handle datasets that are larger than the available memory and to execute complex computational tasks at a much faster rate than traditional methods.

Architecture Overview

The architecture of Dask is composed of multiple interconnected components, each serving a specific purpose in the computational ecosystem. These components include:

High-Level Collections

High-level collections are sophisticated abstractions that closely mimic familiar data structures like NumPy arrays, represented as dask.array, and Pandas DataFrames, represented as dask.dataframe. Additionally, Dask offers dask.bag, which is akin to lists of Python objects. These high-level collections not only support a large subset of functionalities provided by their single-machine equivalents but also enable these operations to be carried out in a parallelized manner. This parallelization is crucial for handling large-scale data and for speeding up computational tasks.

Schedulers

Schedulers play a pivotal role in Dask's architecture. They are tasked with the execution of computations as defined by Dask graphs. Dask offers a variety of schedulers, each fine-tuned for specific computational environments and use-cases. For instance, the "threaded" scheduler is optimized for single-machine computations, making it ideal for local environments. On the other hand, the "distributed" scheduler is designed for cluster-based computations, thereby enabling Dask to operate efficiently in a distributed setting.

Task Graphs

One of the most innovative aspects of Dask is its use of directed acyclic graphs (DAGs) to represent computations. In these task graphs, nodes symbolize either data elements or computational tasks, while the edges signify the dependencies that exist between these tasks. This graphical representation allows Dask to deconstruct complex computations into smaller, more manageable tasks. These tasks can then be executed in parallel, either on a single machine or across a cluster, thereby optimizing resource utilization and reducing computation time.

Architecture Mechanism

When you perform operations on Dask collections, Dask builds a task graph that represents the computation. This graph is a set of tasks with dependencies between them, where each task is a small, deterministic function that takes in inputs and produces outputs.

For example, if you perform a sum operation on a Dask array, Dask would create a task graph that includes tasks to sum the individual chunks of the array and then combine these sums to get the total sum. This graph captures the entire computation but does not execute it immediately. The execution of the task graph is handled by a Dask scheduler. The scheduler takes the task graph and executes the tasks in an order that respects their dependencies. For example, in the sum operation, the tasks to sum the individual chunks of the array would be executed before the task to combine these sums.

Dask's schedulers are designed to execute task graphs in parallel. They can run tasks on multiple threads or processes on a single machine, or on multiple machines in a cluster. The schedulers handle load balancing between different workers and recovery from worker failures. The "threaded" scheduler is a good choice for computations that are mostly NumPy and Pandas operations and fit in memory. It uses a pool of Python threads in a single process and has low overhead. The "distributed" scheduler is a more advanced scheduler that provides additional features like data locality awareness, real-time graphical dashboards, and support for asynchronous programming. It can be used on a single machine or a cluster, and is a good choice for most computations.

Task Scheduling in Dask

Task scheduling is a critical component of Dask's architecture. It's the mechanism that allows Dask to execute complex computations in parallel, making efficient use of computational resources.

Node, Task & Scheduler

In Dask, computations are represented as directed acyclic graphs (DAGs), where each node is a task and edges represent dependencies between tasks. A task is a small, deterministic function that takes inputs and produces outputs. The task graph captures the entire computation but does not execute it immediately. Instead, the execution is handled by a Dask scheduler.

The role of the scheduler is to execute the tasks in the task graph in an order that respects their dependencies. The scheduler can run tasks in parallel on multiple threads or processes, either on a single machine or across a cluster of machines. This is what allows Dask to scale computations beyond the limits of a single machine. Dask provides several schedulers, each optimized for different types of computations and environments. The choice of scheduler can have a significant impact on the performance of your computations.

Threaded Scheduler

The threaded scheduler is Dask's default scheduler for single-machine computations. It uses a pool of Python threads within a single process. This scheduler is a good choice for computations that are mostly NumPy and Pandas operations, as these libraries release the Global Interpreter Lock (GIL) and can effectively utilize multiple cores.

The threaded scheduler has low overhead and can efficiently handle many tasks, but it's not suitable for computations that involve a lot of Python objects or non-GIL-releasing functions, as these can lead to contention and poor performance.

Processes Scheduler

The processes scheduler uses a pool of Python processes instead of threads. This scheduler is a good choice for computations that involve a lot of Python objects or functions that don't release the GIL, as each process has its own Python interpreter and memory space.

However, the processes scheduler has higher overhead than the threaded scheduler, as data needs to be serialized and deserialized when it's passed between processes. This can make it less efficient for computations that involve large amounts of data or many tasks.

Distributed Scheduler

The distributed scheduler is Dask's most advanced scheduler. It can be used on a single machine or a cluster of machines, and it provides a number of advanced features, such as:

- The scheduler takes into account the location of data when scheduling tasks, reducing the amount of data that needs to be transferred between workers.

- The scheduler dynamically prioritizes tasks to minimize computation time and maximize parallelism.

- The scheduler provides real-time graphical dashboards that show the state of the computation and the performance of the workers.

- The scheduler can recover from worker failures, allowing computations to continue even if some workers fail.

The distributed scheduler is a good choice for most Dask computations, as it provides the best performance and the most features. However, it's more complex than the other schedulers and can require more resources to run.

Dask Collection

Dask Collections are a key feature of Dask that allow it to handle large datasets that don't fit into memory. They provide familiar, high-level interfaces that mimic Python's built-in collections and popular libraries like NumPy and Pandas, but allow computations to be performed lazily and in parallel.

We shall now delve into the specifics of Dask Collections and their capabilities.

Dask Arrays

Dask arrays are a core Dask collection that extend NumPy arrays. A Dask array looks and feels a lot like a NumPy array. However, a Dask array doesn't directly hold any data. Instead, it symbolically represents computations over data that is broken up into many small pieces, each of which is a regular NumPy array.

This allows Dask to perform computations on arrays larger than memory by breaking them down into smaller, manageable pieces and executing operations on these pieces in a way that minimizes memory usage. Dask arrays support most of the NumPy interface, using the familiar syntax of NumPy, and computations with Dask arrays are lazily evaluated, meaning they're not computed until the result is explicitly requested.

Dask DataFrames

Dask DataFrames extend Pandas DataFrames to larger-than-memory or distributed environments. A Dask DataFrame is a large parallel DataFrame composed of many smaller Pandas DataFrames, split along the index. These Pandas DataFrames may live on disk for larger-than-memory computing on a single machine, or on many different machines in a cluster.

Like Dask arrays, Dask DataFrames are lazily evaluated and support a large portion of the Pandas API. They're a good choice for data manipulation tasks that are too large for Pandas, and they integrate well with other Dask collections and the broader Python ecosystem.

Dask Bags

Dask bags are a flexible Dask collection for semi-structured data and computations that don't fit neatly into arrays or DataFrames. They implement operations like map, filter, groupby, and aggregations on collections of Python objects.

A Dask bag, often called a "dask.bag" or "db", is a parallel collection of arbitrary Python objects, similar to a PySpark RDD. Dask bags are often used to parallelize simple computations on unstructured or semi-structured data like text data, log files, JSON records, or user-defined Python objects.

Dask Delayed

Dask delayed is a way to parallelize custom code. It allows users to delay function calls into a task graph with dependencies. Dask delayed doesn't provide any fancy parallel algorithms like Dask arrays or Dask DataFrames, but it does give the user complete control over what they want to build. With Dask delayed, you can take existing Python code, make it lazy by delaying the execution of functions, and then Dask will handle the parallel execution for you.

Computational Model in Dask

Dask's computational model is built around task scheduling and parallel execution of those tasks. It's designed to scale from single-machine operations to cluster computing, providing a consistent interface across different computational environments.

We shall now explore the key aspects of Dask's computational model.

Task Graphs

At the heart of Dask's computational model are task graphs. A task graph is a directed acyclic graph (DAG) where nodes represent tasks and edges represent dependencies between tasks. A task is a small, deterministic function that takes inputs and produces outputs.

When you perform operations on Dask collections, Dask builds a task graph that represents the computation. This graph is a set of tasks with dependencies between them. The task graph captures the entire computation but does not execute it immediately. Instead, the execution is handled by a Dask scheduler.

Lazy Evaluation

Dask uses a programming model called lazy evaluation. When you perform operations on Dask collections, the computations are not performed immediately. Instead, Dask records the operations to be performed and builds up a task graph representing the computation.

This has several advantages. First, it allows Dask to optimize the computation before it's executed. Dask can reorder operations, merge tasks, and perform other optimizations to make the computation more efficient. Second, it allows Dask to perform computations in parallel. By breaking the computation down into many small tasks, Dask can execute these tasks on multiple cores or machines at the same time.

Schedulers

The execution of the task graph is handled by a Dask scheduler. The scheduler takes the task graph and executes the tasks in an order that respects their dependencies. The scheduler can run tasks in parallel on multiple threads or processes, either on a single machine or across a cluster of machines.

Dask provides several schedulers, each optimized for different types of computations and environments. The choice of scheduler can have a significant impact on the performance of your computations.

Parallel and Distributed Computing

Dask's computational model is designed to support both parallel and distributed computing. On a single machine, Dask can use multiple cores to execute tasks in parallel, making efficient use of your machine's resources. On a cluster of machines, Dask can distribute tasks across the machines, allowing you to scale your computations beyond the limits of a single machine.

Dask's distributed scheduler provides additional features for distributed computing, such as data locality awareness, dynamic task prioritization, and fault tolerance. These features make Dask a powerful tool for large-scale data analysis and machine learning.

Integration with Python Scientific Stack

Dask is designed to integrate seamlessly with the Python scientific stack. Dask collections provide familiar, high-level interfaces that mimic Python's built-in collections and popular libraries like NumPy and Pandas. This makes it easy to scale existing Python workflows with minimal code changes.

In addition, Dask works well with other Python libraries for parallel and distributed computing, such as Numba for just-in-time compilation and MPI for message passing. This allows you to combine Dask with other tools to build powerful, scalable workflows.

Summary

This chapter provided an introduction to parallel computing with Dask. We first looked at the concept of lazy evaluation, which is key to how Dask works. With lazy evaluation, operations are not executed immediately when called, but instead are stored in a graph to be run later when results are actually needed. This allows Dask to optimize and parallelize computations.

Dask was created to bring flexible parallelism to Python, overcoming limitations of earlier tools like multiprocessing and IPython parallel. Dask provides an architecture for distributed computing on large datasets. Central to this is the task graph, which tracks all the calculations required. Dask can analyze these graphs to efficiently schedule and execute tasks in parallel across resources.

The Dask architecture also includes schedulers that handle how tasks are assigned and executed. Custom schedulers allow Dask to adapt to different environments, from a single machine to large clusters. Collections provide familiar APIs like DataFrames and arrays for operating on large datasets in parallel. By implementing common interfaces like Pandas, Dask makes it easier to transition to parallel computing.

Under the hood, Dask collections utilize blocked algorithms and in-memory caching for fast operations while minimizing memory usage. Coupled with lazy evaluation, this allows efficient computations on datasets larger than memory. The schedulers dynamically load-balance work across threads and processes. Overall, Dask provides a consistent interface for scaling up analyses from a laptop to a distributed cluster.

Chapter 2: Dask Fundamentals

Overview

Chapter 2 is designed to offer an in-depth exploration of Dask's essential elements, equipping you with a robust foundation for harnessing its parallel and distributed computing features. The chapter kicks off with an in-depth look at Dask collections. These are sophisticated data structures that emulate well-known Python entities like lists, arrays, and dataframes. Comprising Dask arrays, Dask dataframes, and Dask bags, these collections offer a user-friendly interface for manipulating large datasets that exceed available memory. Grasping the concept of Dask collections is vital for effective data manipulation in Dask, as they facilitate lazy and parallel computations, optimizing both memory and computational speed.

We then transition into an examination of Dask's computational paradigm. Central to this are task graphs, which depict computations as interrelated tasks with specific dependencies. Dask schedulers oversee the execution of these tasks, enabling parallel processing across multiple threads or processes, whether on a single machine or a distributed network. Comprehending this framework is key to unlocking Dask's full potential for parallel and distributed operations.

The Dask dashboard serves as an invaluable resource for tracking and diagnosing the efficiency of Dask operations. It offers dynamic visual dashboards that display ongoing computations and worker performance. This section will walkthrough you through the effective use of the Dask dashboard to gain valuable insights into your computational tasks and pinpoint performance issues.

Performance profiling is a crucial part of utilizing Dask effectively. It entails evaluating the efficiency of your computations, identifying performance bottlenecks, and fine-tuning your code for optimal speed. This section will introduce you to various techniques for performance profiling within the Dask ecosystem, aiding you in crafting efficient and scalable code.

Managing memory is a critical concern when dealing with extensive datasets in Dask. Dask's lazy evaluation and task scheduling features enable efficient handling of datasets that exceed available memory. This section will delve into Dask's memory management strategies, offering guidance on how to prevent out-of-memory issues and optimize computational tasks.

The chapter concludes with a focus on error management in Dask. As with any software, Dask operations are susceptible to failures due to various errors. Knowing how to manage these errors is essential for developing resilient Dask applications. This section will offer practical approaches for diagnosing and troubleshooting errors within the Dask environment.

In a nutshell, this chapter aims to furnish you with a thorough grasp of the core principles of Dask, empowering you to effectively utilize its capabilities for parallel and distributed computing.

Dask Arrays

We shall revisit Dask arrays to make our understanding as straightforward as possible. Think of a Dask array as a large NumPy array that's been broken down into smaller pieces. Each of these smaller arrays can be processed separately, making it easier to work with huge datasets that might not fit into your computer's memory. Dask arrays are particularly useful when you're dealing with operations that can be performed on each piece independently before combining them back together. This allows for efficient use of computational resources, as tasks can be executed in parallel across multiple CPU cores or even different machines.

So, in essence, a Dask array enables you to perform large-scale array operations without worrying too much about memory limitations or computational inefficiency. It takes care of the heavy lifting in the background, allowing you to focus on your data analysis or scientific computations.

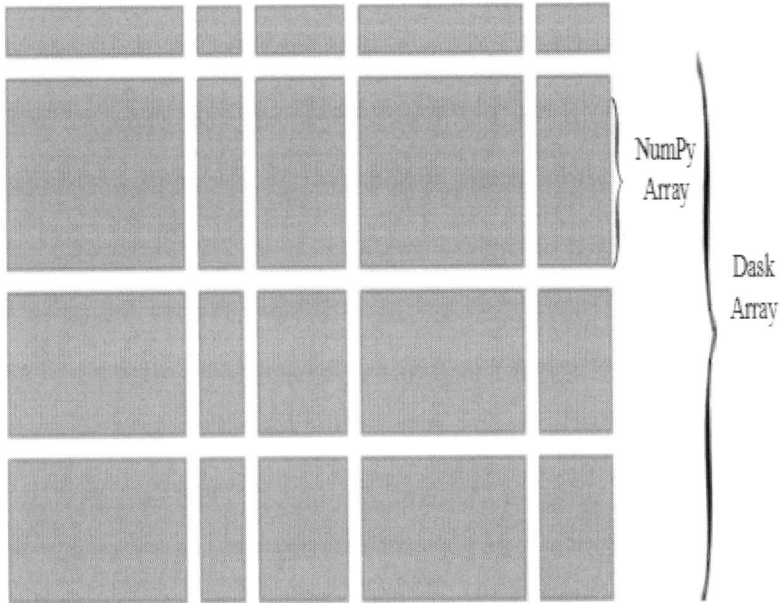

Fig 2.1 Dask Arrays Overview

We shall now dive deeper into Dask arrays and how to work with them. Following is a sequence diagram that illustrates the process:

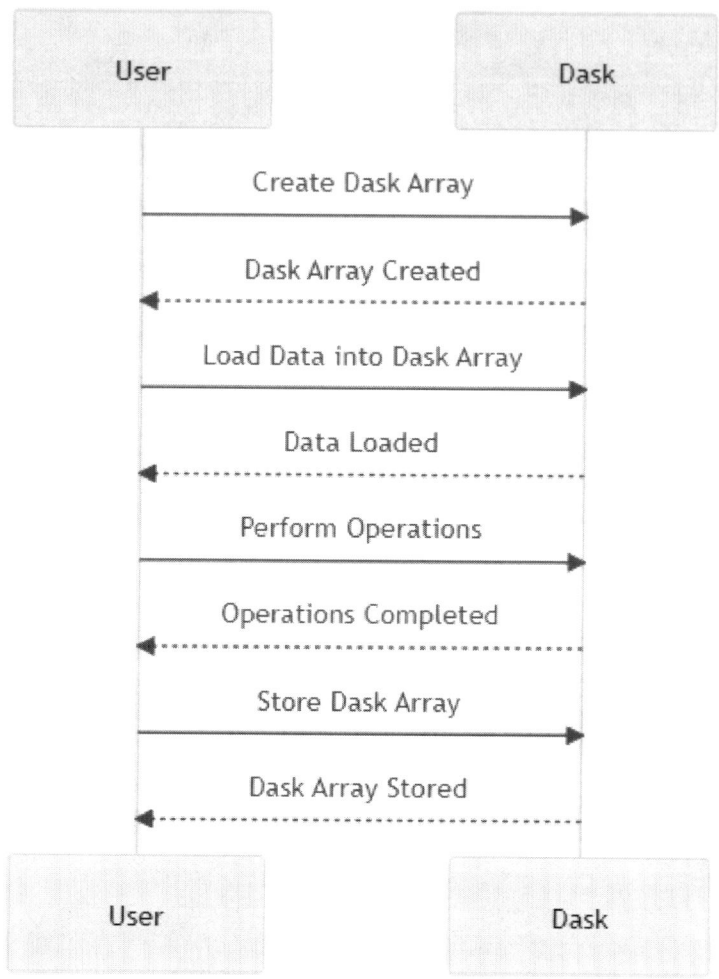

Fig 2.2 Dask Arrays Operations

We shall move on to the practical demonstration.

Creating a Dask Array

First, you need to import Dask array module:

import dask.array as da

You can create a Dask array from a NumPy array using the da.from_array() function. Following is a sample demonstration:

```python
import numpy as np

# Create a NumPy array
numpy_array = np.arange(1000)

# Create a Dask array from the NumPy array
dask_array = da.from_array(numpy_array, chunks=(100,))
```

In the above sample program, the chunks argument specifies the size of the chunks. Dask will divide the array into chunks of this size and compute them separately.

Loading Data into Dask Array

You can load data into a Dask array from various sources, such as a file or a Pandas DataFrame. The given below is a practical illustration of loading data from a CSV file:

```python
import dask.dataframe as dd

# Load data from a CSV file into a Dask DataFrame
df = dd.read_csv('data.csv')

# Convert the Dask DataFrame to a Dask array
dask_array = df.to_dask_array()
```

Performing Operations on Dask Array

You can perform operations on a Dask array just like you would on a NumPy array. Following is a sample demonstration:

```python
# Compute the mean of the Dask array
mean = dask_array.mean().compute()

print(mean)
```

In the above sample program, the compute() function is used to execute the computation. Dask computations are lazy, meaning they're not executed until you explicitly ask for the result.

Storing Dask Array

You can store a Dask array to disk in various formats, such as HDF5 or Zarr. The given below is a practical illustration of storing a Dask array as a HDF5 file:

```
import h5py

# Create a new HDF5 file
with h5py.File('data.h5', 'w') as f:
    # Store the Dask array in the HDF5 file
    dask_array.to_hdf5('data.h5', '/data')
```

In the above sample program, the to_hdf5() function is used to store the Dask array in the HDF5 file. The first argument is the filename, and the second argument is the path in the HDF5 file where the array will be stored. As you can see, Dask arrays provide a familiar interface that's similar to NumPy, but with the added benefit of being able to handle larger-than-memory datasets.

Dask Dataframes

Imagine a Dask dataframe as a gigantic pandas dataframe that's been sliced into smaller, more manageable parts. Each of these smaller dataframes can be operated on independently, making it feasible to work with enormous datasets that exceed your computer's memory capacity.

Just like with Dask arrays, the real power of Dask dataframes comes into play when you have operations that can be executed on each partition separately. This enables parallel processing, allowing you to utilize multiple CPU cores or even distribute the workload across multiple machines.

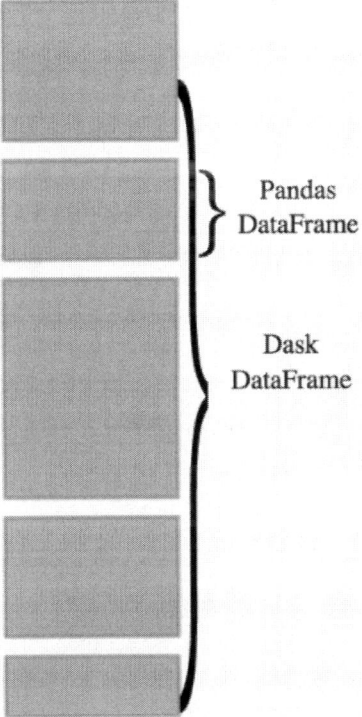

Fig 2.3 Dask DataFrame Overview

We shall now start by understanding Dask DataFrames and how to work with them. The given below is a sequence diagram that illustrates the process:

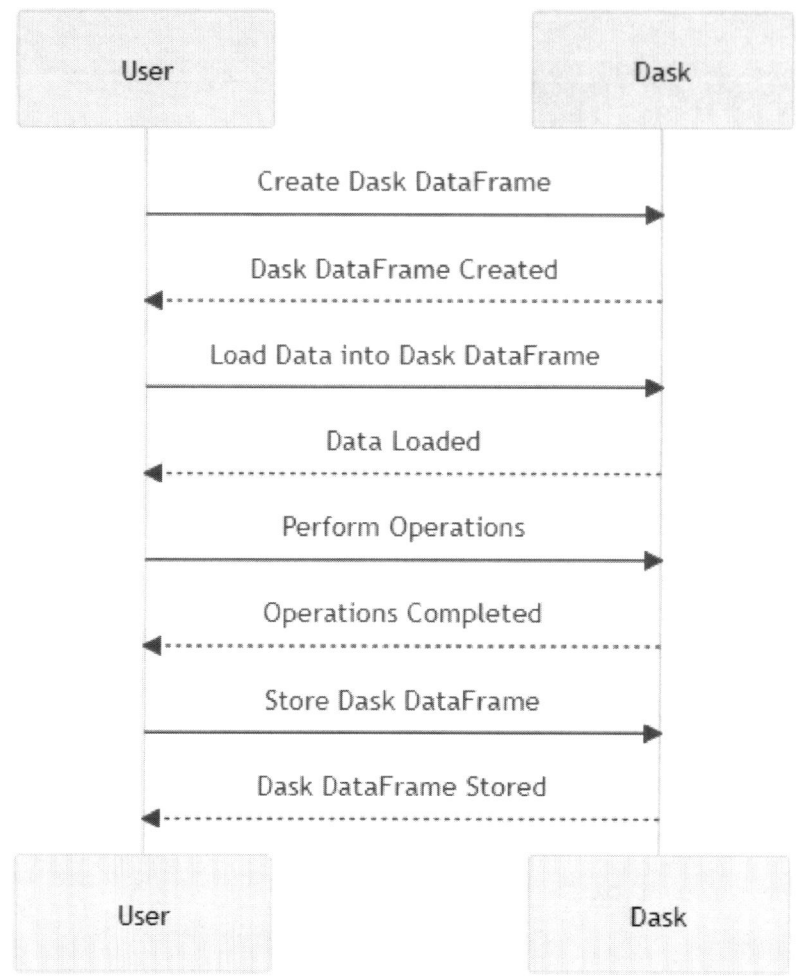

Fig 2.4 Dask DataFrame Operations

We shall move on to the practical demonstration.

Creating Dask DataFrame

First, you need to import Dask DataFrame module:

import dask.dataframe as dd

You can create a Dask DataFrame from a Pandas DataFrame using the dd.from_pandas() function. Following is a sample demonstration:

```python
import pandas as pd

# Create a Pandas DataFrame
pandas_df = pd.DataFrame({
    'x': range(1000),
    'y': range(1000)
})

# Create a Dask DataFrame from the Pandas DataFrame
dask_df = dd.from_pandas(pandas_df, npartitions=10)
```

In the above sample program, the npartitions argument specifies the number of partitions. Dask will divide the DataFrame into partitions and compute them separately.

Loading Data into Dask DataFrame

You can load data into a Dask DataFrame from various sources, such as a file or a database. The given below is a practical illustration of loading data from a CSV file:

```python
# Load data from a CSV file into a Dask DataFrame
dask_df = dd.read_csv('data.csv')
```

Performing Operations on Dask DataFrame

You can perform operations on a Dask DataFrame just like you would on a Pandas DataFrame. Following is a sample demonstration:

```python
# Compute the mean of the 'x' column
mean = dask_df['x'].mean().compute()

print(mean)
```

In the above sample program, the compute() function is used to execute the computation. Dask computations are lazy, meaning they're not executed until you explicitly ask for the result.

Storing Dask DataFrame

You can store a Dask DataFrame to disk in various formats, such as CSV or Parquet. The given below is a practical illustration of storing a Dask DataFrame as a CSV file:

```
# Store the Dask DataFrame as a CSV file
dask_df.to_csv('output.csv')
```

In the above sample program, the to_csv() function is used to store the Dask DataFrame as a CSV file. This is just a simple working with Dask DataFrames.

Dask Bags

Dask Bags, often referred to simply as "bags", are a versatile component of Dask that provide a flexible way to parallelize and distribute computations. Bags are ideal for working with semi-structured data or datasets that do not fit neatly into tables, such as text data or log files. They can be thought of as a parallel and distributed version of Python's lists or iterators, providing many of the same operations as Python's built-in list type, but with the added benefit of being able to operate on large datasets that don't fit into memory.

Bags are unordered collections of arbitrary Python objects, partitioned across multiple machines if running in a distributed environment. Each partition of a bag acts like a small Python list, holding a subset of the total elements. This allows Dask to perform operations on each partition in parallel, greatly improving computational efficiency.

Key Features

One of the key features of bags is their support for functional programming operations, such as map, filter, and reduce. These operations can be chained together to form complex computations. For example, you can use the map function to apply a function to each element of a bag, the filter function to select elements that meet a certain condition, and the reduce function to aggregate elements together.

Bags also support more complex operations, such as groupby and foldby, which can be used to group elements by a key and perform reductions on each group. These operations are similar to the groupby operation in Pandas and SQL, but are designed to work efficiently on large, distributed datasets.

One thing to remember about bags is that they are not as optimized as Dask arrays or Dask DataFrames for certain types of computations. This is because bags have to deal with arbitrary Python objects, which can be more complex and less predictable than the numerical data typically stored in arrays or the tabular data stored in DataFrames. However, bags can be transformed into arrays or DataFrames using the to_array or to_dataframe methods, allowing you to take advantage of the more optimized operations provided by these data structures when appropriate.

In terms of memory management, bags follow the same lazy evaluation model as other Dask collections. This means that computations are not executed until you explicitly ask for the result, allowing Dask to optimize the computation and minimize memory usage.

Performing Dask Bag Operations

Let us start by understanding Dask Bags and how to work with them. The given below is a sequence diagram that illustrates the process:

Fig 2.5 Dask Bag Operations

We shall move on to the practical demonstration.

Creating Dask Bag

First, you need to import Dask bag module:

```
import dask.bag as db
```

You can create a Dask bag from a Python iterable using the db.from_sequence() function. Following is a sample demonstration:

```
# Create a Dask bag from a Python list
bag = db.from_sequence([1, 2, 3, 4, 5], npartitions=2)
```

In the above sample program, the npartitions argument specifies the number of partitions. Dask will divide the bag into partitions and compute on them separately.

Loading Data into Dask Bag

You can load data into a Dask bag from various sources, such as a file or a directory of files. The given below is a practical illustration of loading data from a text file:

```
# Load data from a text file into a Dask bag
bag = db.read_text('data.txt')
```

Performing Operations on Dask Bag

You can perform operations on a Dask bag just like you would on a Python iterable. Following is a sample demonstration:

```
# Compute the sum of the elements in the bag
sum = bag.sum().compute()

print(sum)
```

In the above sample program, the compute() function is used to execute the computation. Dask computations are lazy, meaning they're not executed until you explicitly ask for the result.

Storing Dask Bag

You can store a Dask bag to disk in various formats, such as text or JSON. The given below is a practical illustration of storing a Dask bag as a text file:

```
# Store the Dask bag as a text file
bag.to_textfiles('output-*.txt')
```

In the above sample program, the to_textfiles() function is used to store the Dask bag as a text file. The asterisk (*) in the filename is a wildcard that will be replaced with the partition number.

Dask Delayed

Dask Delayed is a powerful tool that allows you to parallelize your Python code with minimal changes. It's a simple yet effective way to make your code lazy and parallel, which can lead to significant performance improvements when dealing with large datasets or computationally intensive tasks.

The concept behind Dask Delayed is quite simple. When you apply the dask.delayed function to another function or method, it doesn't execute immediately. Instead, it records what you want to compute as a task into a graph that Dask can use to execute your computations in parallel. The real power of Dask Delayed comes when you use it in combination with other Dask collections like arrays, dataframes, and bags. By delaying the computation of these collections, you can build up complex computations by chaining together multiple operations, and then compute the result in one go. This can lead to more efficient use of resources and faster execution times.

Applying Dask Delayed

Let us see how this works in practice with a simple example.

```
import dask

# Define a simple function
def increment(x):
    return x + 1

# Define another simple function
def double(x):
    return x * 2
```

```python
# Define a third function that combines the other two
def add(x, y):
    return x + y

# Use Dask Delayed to make the functions lazy
increment = dask.delayed(increment)
double = dask.delayed(double)
add = dask.delayed(add)

# Now we can use these functions as if they were normal functions
# But the computations are not executed immediately
x = increment(1)
y = double(2)
z = add(x, y)

# The result z is a Dask Delayed object
# We can compute the result with the compute() method
result = z.compute()

print(result)  # prints 5
```

In the above sample program, the increment, double, and add functions are made lazy using dask.delayed. This means that when we call these functions, the computations are not executed immediately. Instead, a Dask Delayed object is returned, which represents the computation that will be performed.

The z.compute() line is where the actual computation happens. Dask executes the computations in parallel, taking care of the dependencies between the tasks. The result is then returned. This is a simple example, but you can imagine how powerful this can be when dealing with more complex computations and larger datasets.

Let us visit the process of the sample program using a sequence diagram:

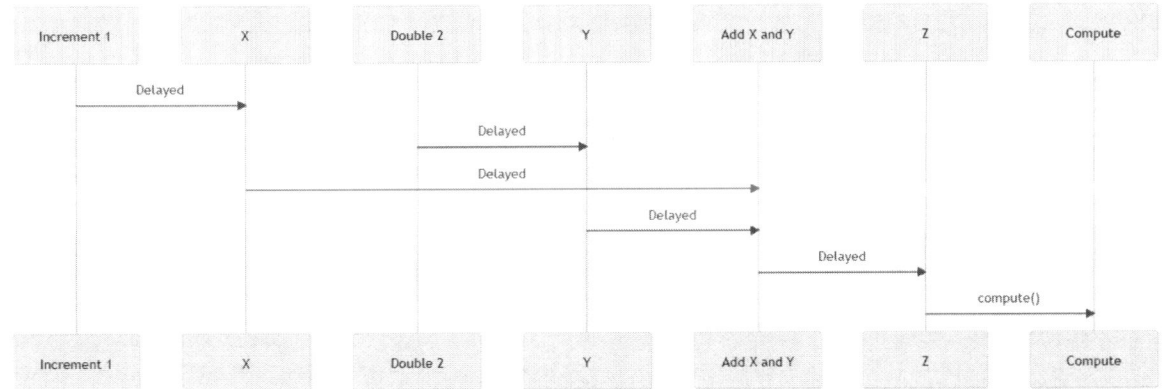

Fig 2.6 Dask Delayed Process

In the diagram, each participant represents a step in the program. The "Increment 1", "Double 2", and "Add X and Y" steps are functions that are made lazy using Dask Delayed. The "X", "Y", and "Z" steps represent the Dask Delayed objects that are returned by these functions. The "Compute" step is where the actual computation happens.

Dask Futures

Dask Futures is a part of Dask that allows for real-time, parallel, and distributed computing. It's an interface that extends Python's concurrent.futures interface, but with additional features for distributed computing. A Future represents a computation that hasn't necessarily completed yet. It's a placeholder for the result of the computation that can be passed around your program, even if the computation is still in progress or hasn't even started yet.

Dask Futures are particularly useful for computations that need to happen in real-time or for computations that have complex dependencies, where you need fine-grained control over the computation order.

Applying Dask Futures

Let us see how this works in practice with a simple example.

```
from dask.distributed import Client, progress
import time

# Start a Dask client
client = Client()
```

```python
# Define a simple function
def increment(x):
    time.sleep(1)  # Simulate a computation that takes time
    return x + 1

# Submit the function to the Dask client
future = client.submit(increment, 1)

# At this point, the computation is happening in the background
# We can check the status of the computation with the progress function
progress(future)

# We can also submit more computations that depend on the result of the first computation
future2 = client.submit(increment, future)

# Again, we can check the status of the computations
progress(future2)

# When we're ready to get the result, we can call the result method
result = future2.result()

print(result)  # prints 3
```

In the above sample program, the increment function is submitted to the Dask client for execution. The client.submit function returns a Future that represents the computation. We can pass this Future around our program, and even submit new computations that depend on the result of the Future.

The progress function is a handy tool that shows the progress of the computations. It's particularly useful when dealing with computations that take a long time to complete. Finally, the result method is used to get the result of the computation. If the computation has not completed yet, this method will block until the result is ready.

Let us simplify the understanding using a sequence diagram:

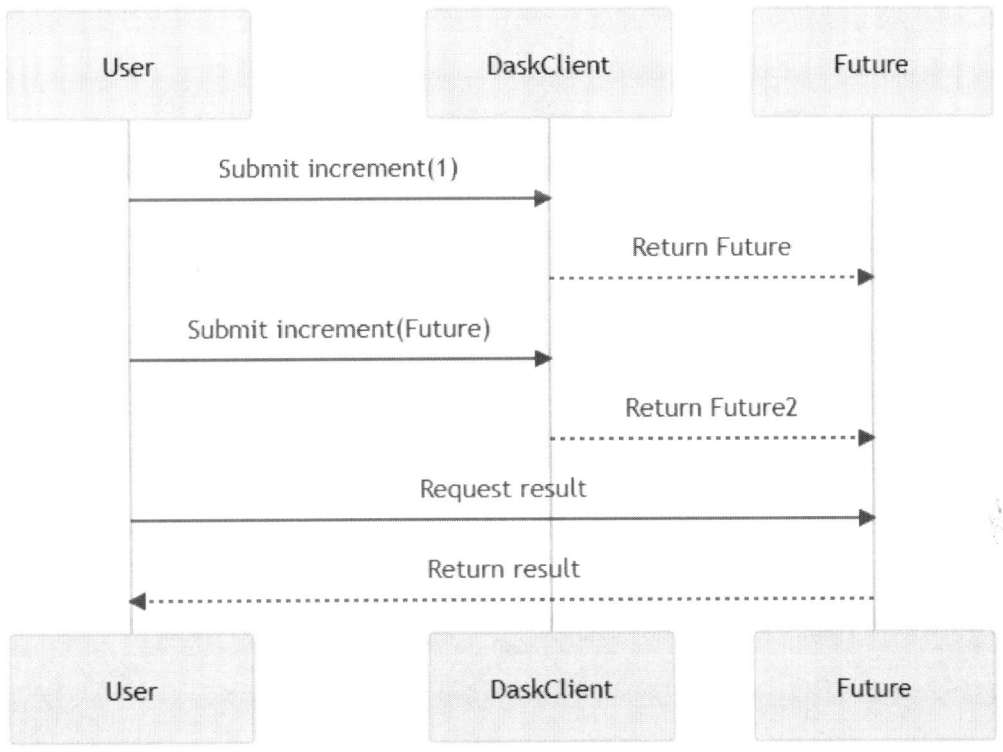

Fig 2.7 Dask Futures Process

In the diagram, each participant represents a step in the program. The "User" submits the increment function to the "DaskClient", which returns a "Future" object. The user then submits another increment function to the "DaskClient" with the "Future" as an argument, which returns another "Future" object. Finally, the user requests the result from the "Future", which returns the result of the computation.

Dask Dashboard

The Dask Dashboard is an indispensable diagnostic utility that offers a real-time, interactive, web-based interface for monitoring the status and performance of your Dask computations. This dashboard serves as a crucial resource for gaining insights into your computations, debugging issues, and fine-tuning performance for optimal results. It is designed to help both novice and experienced users understand the intricacies of Dask's parallel and distributed computing capabilities.

Built upon the robust Bokeh Python library, known for its high-quality interactive visualizations, the Dask Dashboard provides a plethora of visualization options. These visualizations are designed to offer comprehensive insights into various aspects of your Dask computations. The given below is a detailed look at some of the key visualizations you can expect:

Task Stream Visualization

This real-time visualization feature displays the ongoing progress of your computations. Each rectangle in the task stream symbolizes a specific task, and its color coding indicates the nature of the task. The y-axis of this visualization represents the different workers in your computational cluster, while the x-axis denotes the timeline of the computation. This feature is particularly useful for tracking the sequence and status of tasks as they are processed.

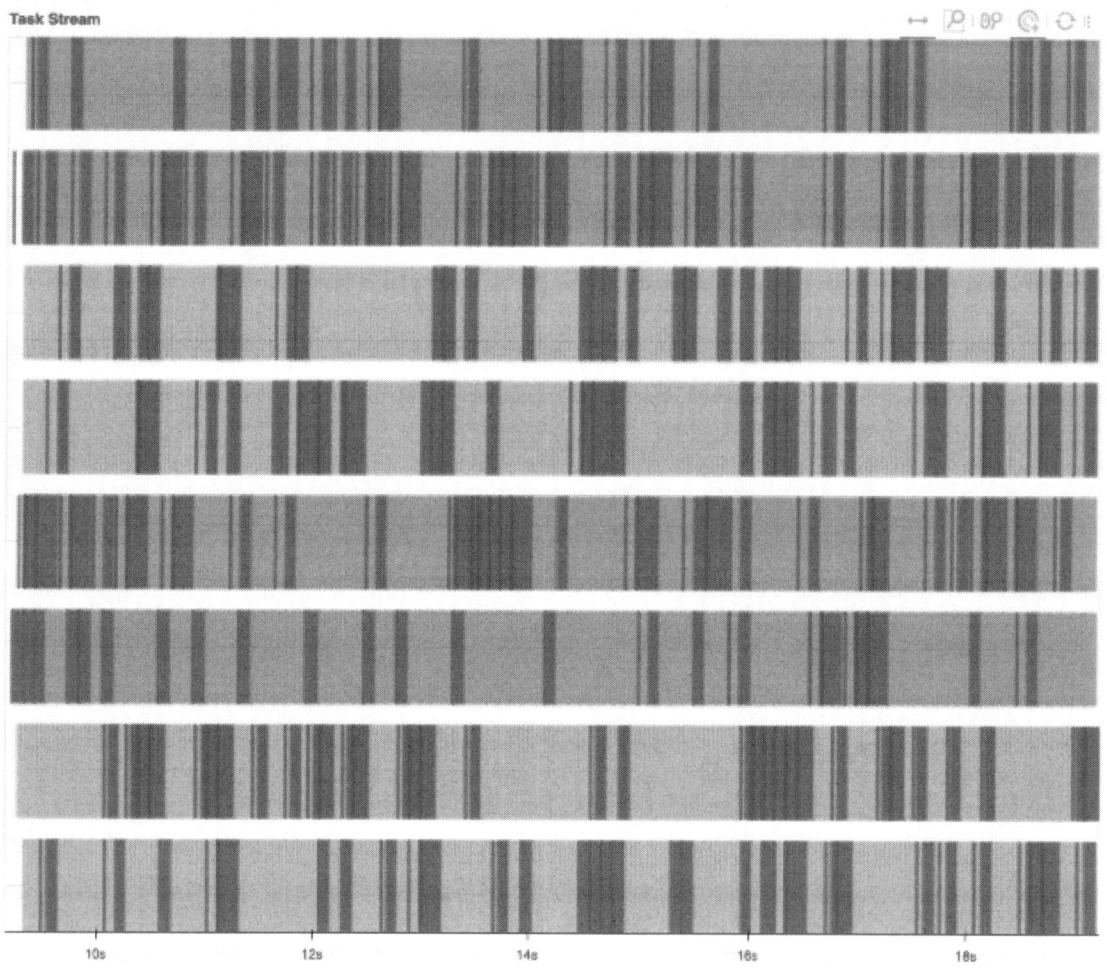

Fig 2.8 Task Stream Visualization

Progress Bar Visualization

This feature offers a straightforward yet effective way to monitor the progress of each type of task involved in your computations. The progress bar gives you a quick overview of the percentage of tasks that have been completed and what remains to be done. It serves as a simple gauge to assess the overall progress of your computational tasks.

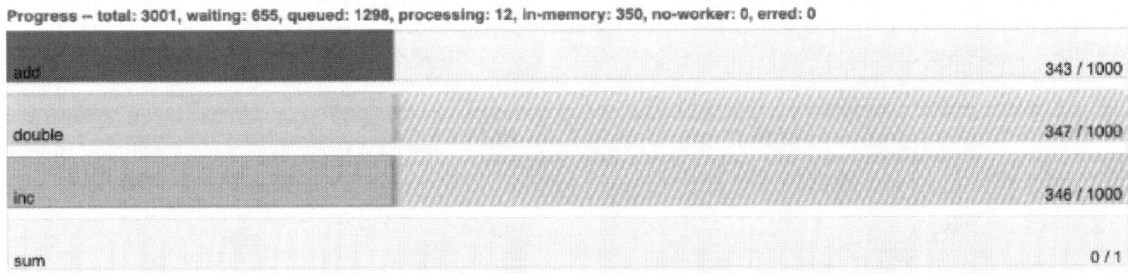

Fig 2.9 Progress Bar Visualization

Memory Usage Visualization

This feature provides a detailed view of the memory consumption by each worker in your cluster. It is an invaluable tool for understanding how your computational tasks are utilizing memory resources. This can be particularly useful for identifying memory-related issues that may arise during the computation, thereby allowing for timely intervention.

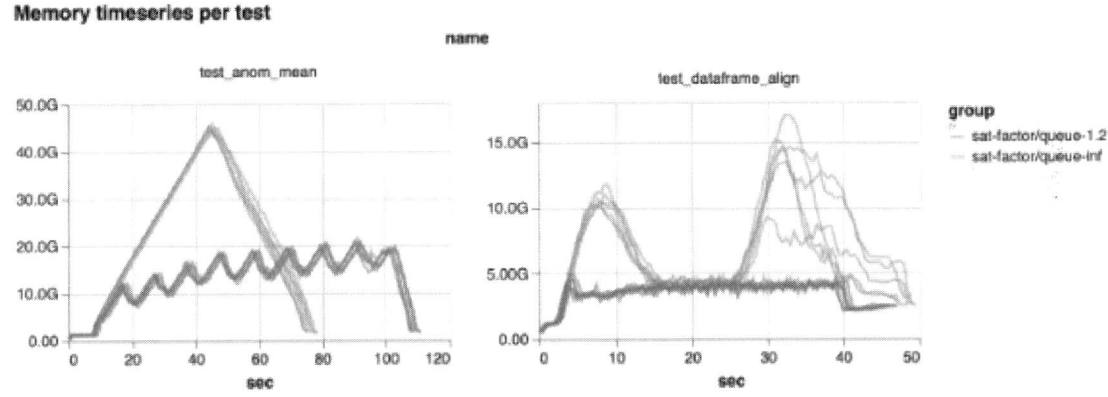

Fig 2.10 Memory Usage Visualization

CPU Usage Visualization

This feature offers insights into the CPU utilization by each worker in your computational cluster. Understanding CPU usage is essential for optimizing the computational efficiency of your tasks. This visualization helps you identify if any worker is underutilized or overburdened, enabling you to make necessary adjustments. The visualization is similar to what is shown for memory usage visuals.

Task Graph Visualization

This is a sophisticated tool that displays the task graph associated with your computation. It helps you understand the dependencies between various tasks and can be instrumental in identifying potential bottlenecks or areas for optimization within your computational workflow.

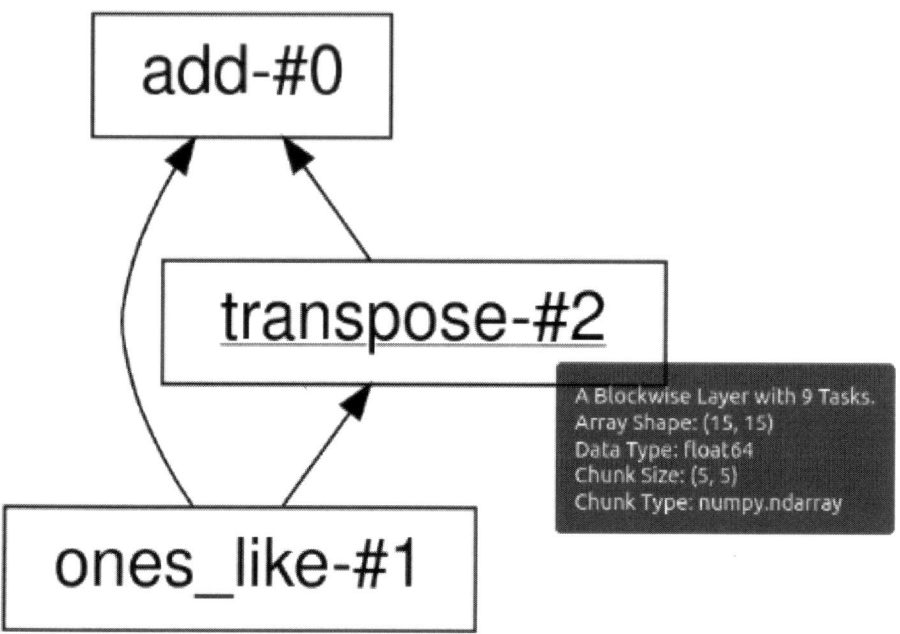

Fig 2.11 Task Graph Visualization

To make use of these extensive features of the Dask Dashboard, you'll first need to initiate a Dask client. Once the client is up and running, it will provide you with a link to access the dashboard. Simply click on the link to open the dashboard in your preferred web browser, and you'll be well on your way to mastering the complexities of Dask computations.

The given below is a simple example:

```
from dask.distributed import Client

# Start a Dask client
client = Client()

# Print the link to the dashboard
print(client.dashboard_link)
```

In the above sample program, the Client object is the entry point to the Dask distributed scheduler. When you create a Client, it starts a local Dask scheduler and worker processes. The dashboard_link attribute of the Client object provides the link to the Dask dashboard. By providing a real-time, interactive view of computations, the Dask dashboard is a powerful tool for understanding, debugging, and optimizing Dask computations

Performance Profiling in Dask

Performance profiling in Dask is a crucial aspect of optimizing your Dask applications. It allows you to understand where your computation is spending time, and helps identify bottlenecks or areas for improvement. Dask provides several tools for performance profiling, including the Dask dashboard mentioned earlier. In addition to the dashboard, Dask also provides the performance_report context manager, which generates an HTML report with a lot of useful information about your computation.

The given below is a practical illustration of how to use performance_report:

```
from dask.distributed import Client, performance_report
import dask.array as da

# Start a Dask client
client = Client()

# Create a large Dask array
x = da.random.random((10000, 10000), chunks=(1000, 1000))

# Use the performance_report context manager to profile the computation
with performance_report(filename="dask-report.html"):
    y = x + x.T
    z = y[::2, 5000:].mean(axis=1)
    z.compute()
```

In the above sample program, we first start a Dask client and create a large Dask array. We then use the performance_report context manager to profile a computation on the array.

The performance_report context manager generates an HTML report that includes a lot of useful information about the computation, including:

- Task stream: A plot showing the execution of tasks over time.

- Task duration: A plot showing the duration of each type of task.

- Worker memory: A plot showing the memory usage of each worker over time.

- Worker CPU: A plot showing the CPU usage of each worker over time.

- Task graph: A visualization of the task graph for the computation.

- Profiler: A detailed breakdown of the time spent in each function during the computation.

The performance_report context manager serves as an impactful instrument for comprehending how well your Dask computations are performing. Offering in-depth insights into the execution process of your tasks, it assists you in pinpointing performance hindrances and potential zones for enhancement.

Dask's Memory Management

Memory management is a critical aspect of optimizing performance in Dask, a parallel computing library in Python. Understanding how Dask handles memory can provide you with the tools to significantly improve the efficiency and speed of your computations.

Below are some of the key strategies and techniques that Dask employs for effective memory management:

- Chunking Strategy for Data Partitioning - In Dask, the concept of "chunking" is fundamental to how it manages large datasets. Rather than attempting to process an entire dataset at once, which could be impractical or impossible due to memory limitations, Dask breaks down the dataset into smaller, more manageable "chunks." Each of these chunks is a subset of your dataset that can be processed independently by Dask. The size and shape of these chunks are configurable and can have a profound impact on both the performance of your computations and the memory footprint. Properly sized chunks verify that the data fits well into memory, thereby reducing the likelihood of memory-related issues.

- Lazy Evaluation for Computational Efficiency - Dask employs a technique known as "lazy evaluation" to enhance computational efficiency. When you define a computation in Dask, it doesn't execute the operation right away. Instead, Dask constructs a "task graph," a data structure that represents the sequence and dependencies of the computation steps. The actual computation is deferred until you explicitly call methods like compute or persist. This deferred execution allows Dask to perform optimizations that can reduce computational time and memory usage. It gives Dask the opportunity to rearrange tasks and combine them in a way that minimizes memory footprint.

- Spilling Data to Disk for Memory Relief - There may be instances where the memory consumption of your Dask workers exceeds available resources. In such cases, Dask has the capability to "spill" data to disk temporarily. This spilling action involves writing portions of the data to the disk to free up valuable memory space. While this is handled automatically by Dask, you also have the flexibility to control the spilling behavior through Dask's configuration settings. This allows you to fine-tune the balance between memory usage and disk I/O based on your specific needs.

- Data Persisting for Repeated Computations - If your computational workflow involves using the same dataset multiple times, Dask offers the persist method to keep this data in memory across computations. By persisting data, you eliminate the need to reload it for each computation, which can result in a significant speed-up. However, it's important to remember that while persisting data can improve computational speed, it does consume more memory. Therefore, it's crucial to use this feature judiciously, especially when working with large datasets.

Sample Program: Automate Management of Memory

The given below is a practical illustration of how to manage memory in Dask:

```
from dask.distributed import Client
import dask.array as da

# Start a Dask client
client = Client()

# Create a large Dask array with small chunks
x = da.random.random((10000, 10000), chunks=(1000, 1000))

# Persist the array in memory
x = x.persist()

# Perform a computation on the array
y = x + x.T
z = y[::2, 5000:].mean(axis=1)
```

```
z.compute()
```

In the above sample program, we first start a Dask client and create a large Dask array with small chunks. We then persist the array in memory using the persist method. This keeps the array in memory, which can speed up subsequent computations on the array. Finally, we perform a computation on the array and call compute to execute the computation.

Error Handling in Dask

Error handling in Dask not only aligns closely with the conventional error-handling paradigms found in standard Python programs but also offers a suite of specialized tools and methodologies. These are designed to assist you in effectively diagnosing and resolving errors that may occur during Dask computations. Understanding these unique aspects can significantly ease the debugging process, making it more efficient and insightful.

Key Aspects of Error Handling in Dask:

- Exceptions and Their Capture: In Dask, when a task within a computation encounters an exception, Dask is designed to capture this exception meticulously. It then raises the exception at the moment you invoke the compute method. Importantly, the exception is accompanied by a detailed traceback, offering you a comprehensive walkthrough to the origin and nature of the error. This traceback can serve as a roadmap for debugging, helping you pinpoint the exact issue swiftly.

- Debugging Techniques: While Dask computations can be debugged using Python's standard debugging utilities like pdb, it's crucial to note that the debugging experience in Dask is somewhat distinct. This is primarily because Dask computations are inherently parallel and distributed across multiple nodes or workers. As a result, the debugging process may require a different approach compared to debugging a monolithic Python application. Understanding these nuances can help you adapt your debugging strategies effectively.

- Role of Dask Dashboard in Debugging: The Dask Dashboard is an invaluable resource when it comes to debugging errors in Dask computations. It offers a plethora of diagnostic information, including but not limited to, a task stream visualization that displays the real-time progress of your computational tasks. Additionally, it features a worker table that provides an overview of the status, including the health and activity, of each worker in your cluster. This information can be instrumental in identifying bottlenecks or issues that may be causing errors.

- Logging Mechanisms: Dask employs Python's built-in logging module to maintain detailed logs of its computational activities. These logs can be an invaluable resource for debugging. You have the flexibility to configure the logging settings to suit your needs. For instance, you can direct the logs to be written to a file, making it easier to review them later. This can be especially useful when you're dealing with complex computations that may produce errors that are not immediately obvious.

- Additional Tools and Techniques: Beyond the standard tools, Dask also offers specialized debugging functionalities tailored for its distributed computing environment. These include options to isolate tasks, examine worker states, and even replay task failures to understand their behavior better. These advanced features can be particularly useful for debugging intricate issues that may not be easily identifiable through conventional methods.

Sample Program: Handling Errors

The given below is a practical illustration of how to handle errors in Dask:

```python
from dask.distributed import Client
import dask.array as da

# Start a Dask client
client = Client()

# Define a function that raises an exception
def raise_exception(x):
    raise Exception("An error occurred!")

# Create a Dask array
x = da.random.random((10000, 10000), chunks=(1000, 1000))

# Apply the function to the array
y = x.map_blocks(raise_exception)

try:
    # Compute the result
    y.compute()
except Exception as e:
    # Handle the exception
```

```
    print("An error occurred during the computation:")
    print(e)
```

In the above sample program, we first start a Dask client and define a function that raises an exception. We then create a Dask array and apply the function to the array using the map_blocks method. When we call compute on the result, Dask executes the computation and raises the exception. We catch the exception using a try/except block and print an error message.

Scenario 1: Division by Zero

In this scenario, you can create a Dask array and perform a division operation that results in a division by zero error.

```
import dask.array as da

# Create a Dask array with a zero
x = da.from_array([1, 2, 0, 3, 4], chunks=2)

# Perform a division operation
y = 1 / x

try:
    # Compute the result
    y.compute()
except ZeroDivisionError as e:
    # Handle the exception
    print("An error occurred during the computation:")
    print(e)
```

In this case, Dask will raise a ZeroDivisionError when it tries to compute the result. We can catch this error and handle it appropriately.

Scenario 2: Invalid Operation

In this scenario, you can try to perform an invalid operation on a Dask array.

```
import dask.array as da
```

```python
# Create a Dask array
x = da.from_array([1, 2, 3, 4, 5], chunks=2)

# Try to perform an invalid operation
y = x + 'a'

try:
    # Compute the result
    y.compute()
except TypeError as e:
    # Handle the exception
    print("An error occurred during the computation:")
    print(e)
```

In this case, Dask will raise a TypeError when it tries to compute the result. We can catch this error and handle it appropriately.

Scenario 3: Out of Memory

In this scenario, you can create a Dask array that is too large to fit into memory.

```python
import dask.array as da

# Create a very large Dask array
x = da.random.random((1000000, 1000000), chunks=(1000, 1000))

try:
    # Compute the result
    x.compute()
except MemoryError as e:
    # Handle the exception
    print("An error occurred during the computation:")
    print(e)
```

In this case, Dask will raise a MemoryError when it tries to compute the result. We can catch this error and handle it appropriately.

The above ones are just a few examples of the types of errors that can occur in Dask computations. The key to handling these errors is to understand the types of exceptions that can be raised and to use Python's standard error handling techniques to catch and handle these exceptions.

Summary

In this chapter, we delved into the fundamentals of Dask, exploring its core components and their functionalities. We started with Dask collections, which are large datasets divided into smaller chunks that can be processed independently. We learned about Dask arrays, dataframes, and bags, and how to create, load, store, and operate on them. We also discovered Dask's lazy evaluation strategy, which allows it to optimize computations and minimize memory usage.

Next, we moved on to Dask's computational model, which is built on task graphs. These graphs represent computations as a set of tasks with dependencies between them, allowing Dask to execute tasks in parallel and distribute them across multiple cores or machines. We also learned about Dask delayed and futures, which are powerful tools for creating custom computations and parallelizing code.

Finally, we explored some of the practical aspects of working with Dask, including performance profiling, memory management, and error handling. We learned how to use the Dask dashboard and the performance_report context manager to understand the performance of our computations. We also learned how Dask manages memory, including how it uses chunking, lazy evaluation, and spilling to disk to handle large datasets. Lastly, we learned how to handle errors in Dask computations, using Python's standard error handling techniques and the additional tools provided by Dask.

Chapter 3: Batch Data Parallel Processing with Dask

Introduction to Batch Processing

Batch processing is a method of executing tasks where data is processed in 'batches' without human intervention. This method of processing is ideal for tasks that do not need immediate action and can be processed in large volumes at a time. Batch processing is a staple in most organizations where large amounts of data need to be processed regularly.

The concept of batch processing comes from the early days of computing when users had to schedule time on mainframe computers to run their tasks. These tasks were then executed as a batch process. Today, batch processing is used in modern computing environments to process high volumes of data where a group of transactions is collected over a period of time. Batch processing systems can handle complex processing instructions, and they are not restricted by manual intervention. This makes them ideal for tasks such as data transformation, where raw data is transformed into a more usable format, or data analysis, where large amounts of data are analyzed to extract meaningful insights.

One of the key applications of batch processing is in the banking and finance industry. Banks process millions of transactions every day. These transactions are collected throughout the day, and then processed in a batch during non-peak hours. This allows banks to optimize their processing power and minimize the impact on their operational systems. Another application of batch processing is in the field of data analytics. Companies collect large amounts of data from various sources. This data is then processed in batches to generate reports, update databases, or feed into machine learning algorithms. By processing the data in batches, companies can verify that their analytics systems are not overwhelmed with data and can operate efficiently.

Batch processing is also used in the healthcare industry. Hospitals and healthcare providers collect vast amounts of patient data. This data is then processed in batches to update patient records, generate reports, or feed into research studies. By using batch processing, healthcare providers can manage their data more efficiently and verify that patient information is up-to-date and accurate. In the field of manufacturing, batch processing is used to control and manage production processes. Data from various stages of the production process is collected and then processed in batches to monitor production efficiency, track inventory, and manage quality control.

Parallel Processing Concepts

Parallel processing is a computational method that allows multiple tasks or processes to be executed simultaneously. This approach leverages the power of modern computing systems, which often have multiple cores or processors, to perform multiple operations at the same time, thereby significantly speeding up computational tasks. The concept of parallel processing is rooted in the idea that large problems can often be divided into smaller ones, which are then solved concurrently.

There are several types of parallelism in computing, including data parallelism, task parallelism, and instruction level parallelism.

- Data Parallelism is a form of parallelism where a large dataset is divided into smaller subsets and the same operation is performed on each subset concurrently. This is particularly useful in tasks such as image or video processing, where the same operation, such as a filter or transformation, can be applied to each pixel or frame independently.

- Task Parallelism, on the other hand, involves breaking down a task into subtasks that can be processed independently and possibly in parallel. This is often used in complex computations where different tasks can be performed concurrently. For example, in a weather forecasting model, different aspects of the model such as temperature, pressure, and humidity calculations can be performed simultaneously.

- Instruction Level Parallelism is a technique used in high-performance computing where individual instructions are executed in parallel. This is typically achieved through pipelining, where different stages of an instruction are executed in parallel, or through superscalar execution, where multiple instructions are executed at the same time.

Parallel processing can significantly speed up computational tasks, but it also introduces complexity in terms of task coordination and data synchronization. For example, when multiple tasks are updating shared data, care must be taken to verify that updates are not lost or that inconsistent states are not observed. This is typically managed through synchronization primitives such as locks or semaphores.

In the context of Dask, parallel processing is a fundamental concept. Dask allows for easy and efficient parallelization of Python code, enabling users to leverage the power of parallel processing without having to deal with the complexities of parallel and distributed computing. Dask does this by creating a task graph of computations to be performed, which can then be executed in parallel on a single machine or across a cluster of machines. Big Data is another area where parallel processing shines. With the exponential growth of data, it's no longer feasible to process large datasets on a single machine. Parallel processing allows us to distribute the data and the processing across multiple machines, enabling us to analyze larger datasets more quickly and efficiently. In the context of Machine Learning and AI, parallel processing is used to train models more quickly. Training a machine learning model involves performing many calculations on large amounts of data. By performing these calculations in parallel, we can train models more quickly, enabling more iterations and ultimately leading to better model performance.

However, parallel processing is not without its challenges. One of the main challenges is coordinating the execution of tasks and managing shared resources. This can lead to issues such as race conditions, where the output is dependent on the sequence of execution, or deadlocks, where two or more tasks are each waiting for the other to release a resource. Another challenge is the distribution of data. In a parallel system, data needs to be distributed across multiple processors or machines. This distribution needs to be balanced to verify that all processors are working efficiently and that no single processor becomes a bottleneck. Despite these challenges, the benefits of parallel processing in terms of speed and efficiency often outweigh the complexities. With tools like Dask, these complexities are largely abstracted away.

Parallel Batch Processing Procedure

Parallel batch processing is a technique that allows you to process large amounts of data more efficiently by dividing the data into smaller batches and processing these batches in parallel.

Following are the broad steps involved in parallel batch processing:

- Data Partitioning: The first step in parallel batch processing is to divide your data into smaller, manageable batches. This process is known as data partitioning. The goal here is to create partitions that can be processed independently of each other. The size of these partitions can vary depending on the nature of the data and the processing requirements. It's important to verify that the data within each partition is related in a way that makes sense for the processing task at hand.

- Task Definition: Once the data is partitioned, the next step is to define the tasks that need to be performed on each batch of data. This could be anything from a simple transformation operation to a complex machine learning algorithm. The key here is that the task should be able to run independently on each batch of data.

- Task Distribution: After defining the tasks, the next step is to distribute these tasks across multiple processors or machines. This is where the parallel aspect of parallel batch processing comes into play. Each processor or machine takes a batch of data and the associated task, and processes the batch independently of the others. This distribution of tasks can be managed manually, but in most cases, it's handled by a task scheduling system.

- Task Execution: Once the tasks are distributed, they are then executed in parallel. Each processor or machine works on its batch of data, executing the task and producing a result. This is where the speedup from parallel batch processing comes from - instead of processing the data sequentially, the data is processed in parallel, significantly reducing the overall processing time.

- Result Aggregation: After all the tasks have been executed, the results from each task need to be aggregated. This could involve simply collecting the results from each task, or it could involve some form of reduction operation, such as summing the results or finding the maximum or minimum value.

- Post-Processing: Once the results have been aggregated, there may be some post-processing required. This could involve transforming the results into a desired format, storing the results in a database, or using the results to make decisions or predictions.

- Error Handling: Throughout this process, it's important to have robust error handling in place. This involves monitoring the execution of the tasks, handling any errors that occur, and ensuring that the system can recover from errors in a graceful manner.

These above are the broad steps involved in parallel batch processing. The specifics of each step can vary greatly depending on the nature of the data, the processing requirements, and the computing environment. However, these steps provide a general framework that can be adapted to a wide range of parallel batch processing scenarios.

Sample Program: Perform Batch Processing

Let us consider a realistic example where we have a large dataset of customer reviews for a product, and we want to perform sentiment analysis on these reviews. The dataset is too large to process on a single machine, so you can use Dask to perform parallel batch processing.

First, we need to partition our data. With Dask, we can do this using Dask DataFrames, which are a large parallel DataFrame composed of many smaller pandas DataFrames, split along the index. These pandas DataFrames may live on disk for larger-than-memory computing on a single machine, or on many different machines in a cluster. One Dask DataFrame operation triggers many operations on the constituent pandas DataFrames.

```
import dask.dataframe as dd

# Load the data into a Dask DataFrame
df = dd.read_csv('reviews.csv')
```

This will create a Dask DataFrame where each partition is a subset of the original DataFrame

Next, we define the task that we want to perform on each batch of data. In this case, we want to perform sentiment analysis on the review text. We can define a function to do this:

```
from textblob import TextBlob

def analyze_sentiment(text):
    return TextBlob(text).sentiment.polarity
```

With Dask, task distribution is handled automatically. We simply apply our function to the DataFrame, and Dask takes care of distributing the tasks:

```python
# Apply the function to the 'review_text' column
df['sentiment'] = df['review_text'].apply(analyze_sentiment, meta=('review_text', 'float64'))
```

To execute the tasks, we call the compute method on the DataFrame. This tells Dask to execute the computation and return the result:

```python
result = df.compute()
```

In this case, our result is a new DataFrame with a 'sentiment' column. We might want to aggregate this result to get the average sentiment:

```python
average_sentiment = result['sentiment'].mean()
print(average_sentiment)
```

Post-processing will depend on what you want to do with the results. In this case, we might want to save the results back to a CSV file:

```python
result.to_csv('sentiment_analysis.csv')
```

Throughout this process, it's important to handle any errors that might occur. This could involve wrapping our code in try/except blocks, checking the status of the computation, or using Dask's built-in diagnostics.

```python
try:
    result = df.compute()
except Exception as e:
    print("An error occurred:", e)
```

This is a basic example of how you might use Dask to perform parallel batch processing. The specifics will depend on your particular use case and computing environment.

Applying Dask on Large Dataset

We shall explore another different scenario. In this instance, you can employ Dask to execute a parallelized computation on an extensive dataset containing weather information. Our objective will be to determine the monthly average temperature.

Data Partitioning

First, we need to load our data. You can use Dask's DataFrame, which can handle larger-than-memory datasets by breaking them into smaller, manageable pieces.

```
import dask.dataframe as dd

# Load the data into a Dask DataFrame
df = dd.read_csv('weather_data.csv')
```

Task Definition

Next, we define the task that we want to perform on each partition of data. In this case, we want to calculate the average temperature for each month. We can define a function to do this:

```
def calculate_monthly_average(df):
    # Convert the 'date' column to datetime
    df['date'] = dd.to_datetime(df['date'])

    # Extract the month from the date
    df['month'] = df['date'].dt.month

    # Group by month and calculate the average temperature
    monthly_average = df.groupby('month')['temperature'].mean()

    return monthly_average
```

Task Distribution

With Dask, task distribution is handled automatically. We simply apply our function to the DataFrame:

```
# Apply the function to the DataFrame
result = calculate_monthly_average(df)
```

Task Execution

To execute the tasks, we call the compute method:

```
result = result.compute()
```

Result Aggregation

In this case, our result is a Series with the average temperature for each month. We might want to convert this to a DataFrame and save it to a CSV file:

```
# Convert to DataFrame
result_df = result.to_frame()

# Reset the index
result_df = result_df.reset_index()

# Rename the columns
result_df.columns = ['month', 'average_temperature']

# Save to CSV
result_df.to_csv('monthly_average_temperature.csv', index=False)
```

Error Handling

As before, it's important to handle any errors that might occur. This could involve wrapping our code in try/except blocks, checking the status of the computation, or using Dask's built-in diagnostics.

```
try:
    result = result.compute()
except Exception as e:
    print("An error occurred:", e)
```

This above example demonstrates how we can use Dask to perform complex operations on large datasets in parallel.

Introduction to Dask Partitioning

Data partitioning is a key concept in parallel and distributed computing. It refers to the process of dividing a large dataset into smaller, manageable chunks, or partitions, that can be processed independently. This allows for the workload to be distributed across multiple processors or nodes in a cluster, enabling parallel processing and thus, potentially, significant improvements in computational speed.

In the context of Dask, data partitioning is handled automatically when you create a Dask collection like a Dask Array or a Dask DataFrame. These collections are designed to operate on larger-than-memory datasets by breaking them down into smaller, manageable pieces, and then executing operations on these pieces in parallel. When you create a Dask DataFrame, for example, you're actually creating a large, logical DataFrame composed of many smaller pandas DataFrames. These smaller DataFrames, or partitions, can be processed independently of each other, which allows Dask to distribute the computation across multiple cores or even multiple nodes in a cluster.

The given below is a practical illustration of how you might create a Dask DataFrame from a large CSV file:

```python
import dask.dataframe as dd

# Load a large CSV file into a Dask DataFrame
df = dd.read_csv('large_dataset.csv')
```

In the above sample program, dd.read_csv works much like pandas.read_csv, but instead of loading the entire dataset into memory at once, it loads the data in partitions, creating a Dask DataFrame. Each partition is a regular pandas DataFrame that can fit comfortably in memory.

The number of partitions is determined automatically based on the size of your dataset and the amount of memory available, but you can also specify it manually if you prefer. Each partition can be processed independently, which allows Dask to distribute the computation across multiple cores or nodes. Once the data is partitioned, you can perform operations on the Dask DataFrame just like you would with a pandas DataFrame. Dask takes care of scheduling these operations to run on the individual partitions in parallel, handling interdependencies between tasks, and aggregating the results.

Determining Partitions

You can manually specify the number of partitions when creating a Dask DataFrame. This can be useful if you have specific knowledge about your dataset or your computing environment that Dask's automatic partitioning might not take into account.

The given below is how you can do it:

```
import dask.dataframe as dd

# Load a large CSV file into a Dask DataFrame with a specific number of partitions

df = dd.read_csv('large_dataset.csv', blocksize='500MB')

# blocksize determines the size of each partition
```

In the above sample program, the blocksize parameter determines the size of each partition. Dask will try to create partitions that are approximately this size. The size can be specified as a string (like '500MB') or as an integer (the number of bytes). Keep in mind that the optimal number of partitions can depend on a variety of factors, including the size of your dataset, the amount of memory available, the nature of your computation, and the number of cores or nodes in your cluster. As a general rule of thumb, you might want to aim for partitions that are small enough to fit comfortably in memory but large enough to keep all your cores or nodes busy.

Also, remember that while manually specifying the number of partitions can sometimes improve performance, in many cases Dask's automatic partitioning will be sufficient and you won't need to adjust it.

Let us say you have a function that performs some operation on the DataFrame:

```
def perform_operation(df):
    # Perform some operation on the DataFrame
    df['new_column'] = df['existing_column'].apply(some_function)
    return df
```

You can then apply this function to each partition of the DataFrame using the map_partitions method:

```
# Apply the function to each partition
df = df.map_partitions(perform_operation)
```

In the above sample program, the perform_operation function will be applied to each partition independently, allowing for parallel processing.

Task Graphs

Task graphs are a fundamental concept in Dask. They are a visual representation of the computations that Dask needs to perform to achieve a certain result. Each node in the graph represents a task, and the edges represent the dependencies between tasks.

The purpose of task graphs is twofold:

1. Scheduling: Task graphs are used by Dask's scheduler to determine the order in which tasks should be executed. Tasks without dependencies can be executed in parallel, while tasks with dependencies need to be executed in a specific order.

2. Debugging and Optimization: Task graphs can be used to understand the computation and to identify potential areas for optimization. By looking at the task graph, you can see which tasks are taking the most time, which tasks are being executed in parallel, and where there might be opportunities to reduce computation.

We shall see how to visualize and optimize task graphs using Dask. You can continue with the previous example of a Dask DataFrame:

```
import dask.dataframe as dd

# Load a large CSV file into a Dask DataFrame
df = dd.read_csv('large_dataset.csv', blocksize='500MB')

# Define a function to perform some operation
def perform_operation(df):
    df['new_column'] = df['existing_column'].apply(lambda x: x**2)
    return df

# Apply the function to each partition
df = df.map_partitions(perform_operation)
```

To visualize the task graph, you can use the visualize method:

```
df.visualize(filename='task_graph.png')
```

This will generate an image of the task graph and save it as 'task_graph.png'. Each box in the graph represents a task, and the arrows represent dependencies between tasks. To optimize the task graph, you can use the persist method. This method tells Dask to execute the tasks and keep the results in memory, which can speed up subsequent computations:

```
df = df.persist()
```

After calling persist, you can visualize the task graph again to see the effect of the optimization:

```
df.visualize(filename='optimized_task_graph.png')
```

In this optimized task graph, you should see fewer tasks, as some of them have been combined or eliminated. This can lead to more efficient computation, especially for complex workflows with many tasks and dependencies.

Summary

In this chapter, we took a deep dive into the realm of batch processing, focusing on its effective execution through Dask. We initiated our learnings by recognizing the critical importance of batch processing, particularly when dealing with voluminous datasets that exceed the limitations of available memory. We came to understand that the essence of batch processing lies in decomposing large-scale tasks into smaller, more manageable sub-tasks. This division not only facilitates parallel processing but also optimizes the utilization of computational power.

Subsequently, we ventured into the core elements of Dask, encompassing Dask Arrays, Dask DataFrames, Dask Bags, Dask Delayed, and Dask Futures. We delved into the methods for creating, loading, and manipulating these specialized Dask collections. These collections are particularly advantageous for working with datasets that are too large to fit into memory; they partition these datasets into smaller chunks that can be processed concurrently. Additionally, we examined Dask's unique computational model. This model empowers us to construct intricate computations as a sequence of interrelated, smaller tasks. We also learned how Dask's internal scheduler intelligently determines the most efficient sequence for task execution, taking into account their interdependencies.

To conclude, we turned our attention to the diagnostic utilities offered by Dask, such as the Dask Dashboard and performance profiling features. These tools offer invaluable insights into the real-time execution of our Dask-based computations, aiding us in pinpointing potential performance bottlenecks or areas that could benefit from optimization. We also touched upon the topics of memory management and error mitigation within the Dask environment. We learned strategies for dealing with prevalent errors to verify that our computational processes are both robust and reliable. Through a series of practical demonstrations and interactive exercises, we acquired a more profound comprehension of how Dask can be harnessed for efficient and scalable batch processing.

Chapter 4: Distributed Systems and Dask

Distributed Systems Overview

Distributed systems are a collection of independent computers that appear to the users of the system as a single coherent system. In other words, a distributed system is one where a collection of independent nodes is made to work together towards a common goal, thus functioning as a single system to the end user. These nodes, or computers, communicate and coordinate their actions by passing messages to each other over a network.

The primary goal of a distributed system is to make it easy for a collection of machines to work together to provide a useful service or solve a complex problem that a single machine may not be able to handle. This can involve sharing resources, improving performance, providing redundancy or fault tolerance, or enabling geographically dispersed collaboration. Distributed computing is the field of computer science that studies distributed systems. In distributed computing, a single problem is divided into many tasks, each of which can be solved by one or more computers in the system. The results of these tasks are then combined to produce the final result.

Python, being a versatile and powerful language, has several libraries and frameworks that support distributed computing. Dask, which we have been exploring in detail, is one of them. Dask allows for parallel and distributed computing in Python by enabling you to work with larger-than-memory datasets and perform complex computations by breaking them down into smaller tasks that can be executed in parallel. Another popular tool for distributed computing in Python is Apache Spark, which provides high-level APIs for distributed data processing. PySpark is the Python library for Spark that lets you harness the power of Spark while working with Python. Celery is another distributed task queue in Python. It's a robust and flexible tool that lets you distribute work across threads or machines. Ray is a high-performance distributed execution framework targeted at large-scale machine learning and reinforcement learning applications. It includes a powerful API for distributed task programming.

In distributed computing, it's important to consider factors like data distribution, load balancing, fault tolerance, and consistency. Data distribution involves deciding how to distribute the data across the nodes in the system. Load balancing assures that all nodes in the system do approximately an equal amount of work. Fault tolerance is the ability of a system to continue functioning in the event of a failure of some of its components. Consistency, in a distributed system, involves ensuring that all nodes see the same data at the same time.

In the following sections, we will explore these concepts in more detail and learn how to implement distributed computing in Python using Dask and other tools. We will also learn about key distributed system concepts that are crucial for working with Dask and other distributed computing frameworks.

Understanding Distributed Scheduler in Dask

The Dask distributed scheduler is a key component of Dask that enables it to execute computations in parallel across multiple cores or machines. It is a centrally managed, distributed, dynamic task scheduler. The distributed scheduler is more sophisticated than the simpler schedulers provided by Dask and is necessary for scaling work across multiple nodes or for dealing with complex computations. The Dask distributed scheduler works by coordinating the execution of tasks in a Dask computation. It does this by tracking the dependencies between tasks and ensuring that tasks are executed in the correct order, and that the results of tasks are available where and when they are needed.

The architecture of the Dask distributed scheduler involves three main components:

1. Scheduler: The scheduler is the central hub that manages the computation. It keeps track of all tasks, their dependencies, and their state (whether they are waiting to be executed, currently being executed, or have already been executed). The scheduler makes decisions about when and where to run tasks based on their dependencies and the current state of the computation.

2. Workers: Workers are the entities that perform the actual computation. They execute tasks as directed by the scheduler and store the results. Each worker is a separate process that can be located on the same machine as the scheduler or on a different machine. In a distributed system, you would typically have multiple workers spread across multiple machines.

3. Client: The client is the user-facing entry point to the Dask distributed scheduler. It is used to define computations and submit them to the scheduler for execution. The client communicates with the scheduler, submitting tasks and retrieving results.

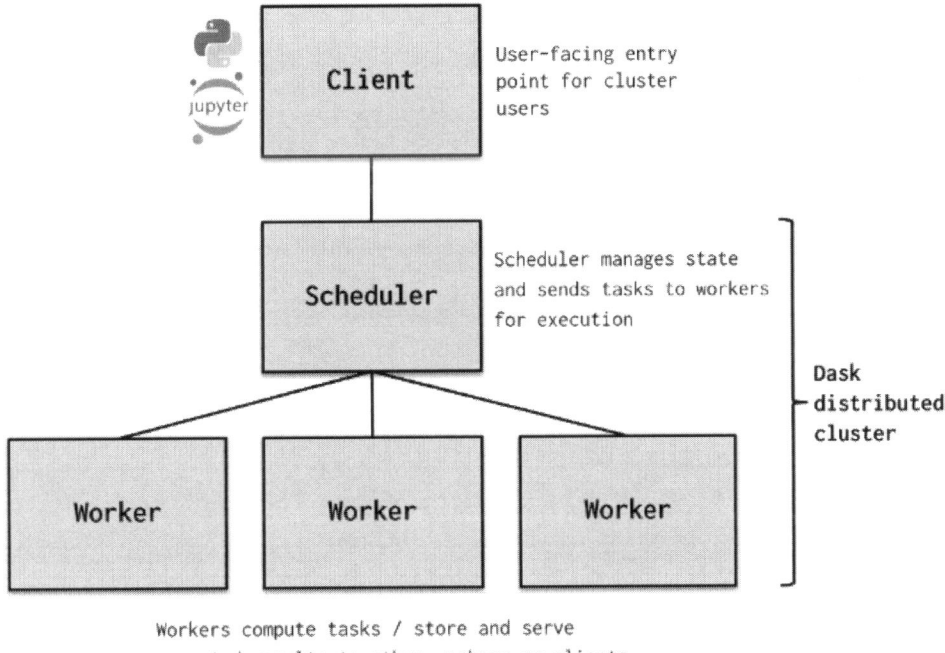

Fig 4.1 Dask Distributed Scheduler

The given below is how it works:

- When you define a Dask computation (for example, by creating a Dask DataFrame and performing some operation on it), Dask translates this computation into a series of tasks with dependencies between them. This is represented as a directed acyclic graph (DAG).

- When you call compute on a Dask object, the computation is sent to the client, which sends the tasks to the scheduler. The scheduler then assigns these tasks to workers for execution, taking into account their dependencies.

- As the workers execute the tasks, they communicate with the scheduler to report progress and to receive new tasks to execute. The scheduler keeps track of which tasks have been completed and where their results are stored.

- Once all tasks have been executed, the final result is sent back to the client.

The Dask distributed scheduler is designed to be highly flexible and can handle a wide range of workloads. It is also robust and can recover from failures of individual tasks or workers. This makes it a powerful tool for executing complex, large-scale computations in Python.

Configure Distributed Cluster

A Dask distributed cluster is a group of machines that work together to perform computations. The cluster consists of one scheduler and one or more workers. The scheduler coordinates the execution of tasks, while the workers perform the actual computations. The machines in a Dask cluster can be located on the same local network or spread across multiple networks.

Setting up and running a Dask distributed cluster involves the following steps:

Install Dask Distributed

The first step is to install the Dask distributed library on all machines that will be part of the cluster. This can be done using pip or conda:

```
pip install dask[distributed]
```

or

```
conda install dask distributed -c conda-forge
```

Start Scheduler

On the machine that you want to act as the scheduler, you start the scheduler using the dask-scheduler command. This will print out the address of the scheduler, which you will need to connect the workers and the client.

```
dask-scheduler
```

Start Workers

On each machine that you want to act as a worker, you start a worker using the dask-worker command, followed by the address of the scheduler:

```
dask-worker <scheduler-address>
```

Connect Client

In your Python script or notebook, you create a Client object and connect it to the scheduler:

```
from dask.distributed import Client
```

```
client = Client('<scheduler-address>')
```

We shall see how to use a Dask distributed cluster with a practical example. You can continue with the previous example of a Dask DataFrame:

```
import dask.dataframe as dd

# Load a large CSV file into a Dask DataFrame
df = dd.read_csv('large_dataset.csv', blocksize='500MB')

# Define a function to perform some operation
def perform_operation(df):
    df['new_column'] = df['existing_column'].apply(lambda x: x**2)
    return df

# Apply the function to each partition
df = df.map_partitions(perform_operation)

# Call compute to start the computation
result = df.compute()
```

When you call compute, Dask automatically uses the distributed scheduler and the cluster that you set up. The computation is divided into tasks that are sent to the scheduler, which assigns them to the workers. The workers execute the tasks and send the results back to the scheduler, which collects them and sends the final result back to the client.

Monitor Dask Clusters

Monitoring a Dask distributed cluster is crucial for understanding the performance of your computations and identifying potential bottlenecks. Dask provides several tools for monitoring, including the Dask dashboard, which provides a real-time, interactive web interface for tracking the progress of computations, the state of the cluster, and more.

To access the Dask dashboard, you simply open a web browser and navigate to the address of the scheduler, followed by the port number 8787. For example, if your scheduler is running on localhost, you would navigate to http://localhost:8787.

The Dask dashboard provides several views, including:

- Task Stream: This shows the progress of tasks as they are being executed by the workers. Each task is represented by a rectangle, and the color of the rectangle indicates the type of task.

- Progress: This shows a high-level summary of the progress of the computation, including the number of tasks completed, in progress, and remaining.

- Workers: This shows information about each worker in the cluster, including its memory usage, CPU usage, and number of tasks in progress.

- System: This shows system-level metrics such as CPU and memory usage for the entire cluster.

- Graph: This shows the task graph for the current computation, with nodes representing tasks and edges representing dependencies between tasks.

- Profile: This shows a performance profile of the computation, with information about the time spent in each function.

We shall now see how to use the Dask dashboard with a practical example and that too the same previous example of a Dask DataFrame:

```
from dask.distributed import Client
import dask.dataframe as dd

# Connect to the Dask distributed cluster
client = Client('<scheduler-address>')

# Load a large CSV file into a Dask DataFrame
df = dd.read_csv('large_dataset.csv', blocksize='500MB')

# Define a function to perform some operation
def perform_operation(df):
    df['new_column'] = df['existing_column'].apply(lambda x: x**2)
    return df
```

```
# Apply the function to each partition
df = df.map_partitions(perform_operation)

# Call compute to start the computation
result = df.compute()
```

While this computation is running, you can open the Dask dashboard in your web browser and monitor the progress of the computation in real-time. You can see which tasks are being executed, how much memory is being used, and more.

Distributed Task Scheduling

Task scheduling in distributed systems is a critical aspect of ensuring efficient execution of computations. In the context of Dask, task scheduling is the process by which the Dask scheduler assigns tasks to workers for execution. The goal of the scheduler is to minimize the total computation time, while also ensuring that tasks are executed in the correct order based on their dependencies.

In a Dask distributed system, the scheduler uses a dynamic task scheduling strategy, which means that it makes scheduling decisions on-the-fly as tasks are completed and new tasks become ready to execute. This is in contrast to static task scheduling, where all scheduling decisions are made upfront before the computation begins.

Given below is how task scheduling works in a Dask distributed system:

- Task Graph Generation: When you define a Dask computation, Dask generates a task graph, which is a directed acyclic graph (DAG) that represents the computation. Each node in the graph represents a task, and each edge represents a dependency between tasks.

- Task Submission: When you call compute on a Dask object, the tasks in the task graph are submitted to the scheduler. The scheduler keeps track of the state of each task (whether it is waiting to be executed, currently being executed, or has already been executed).

- Task Assignment: The scheduler assigns tasks to workers for execution. It does this based on the dependencies between tasks and the current state of the computation. The scheduler tries to assign tasks to workers in a way that minimizes data transfer between workers. For example, if a task depends on the result of another task that was executed on a particular worker, the scheduler will try to assign the task to the same worker.

- Task Execution: The workers execute the tasks as directed by the scheduler. As each task is completed, the worker sends the result back to the scheduler and receives a new task to execute.

- Task Reassignment: If a worker fails or becomes unavailable, the scheduler can reassign its tasks to other workers. This makes Dask resilient to failures and allows it to continue the computation even if some workers fail.

- Result Collection: Once all tasks have been executed, the scheduler collects the results and sends them back to the client.

The Dask scheduler uses several strategies to optimize task scheduling as explained in the next section.

Optimization Strategies for Task Scheduling

Optimizing task scheduling in a distributed system like Dask is crucial for ensuring efficient execution of computations. The Dask scheduler uses several strategies to optimize task scheduling:

- Work Stealing: This is a strategy where idle workers can "steal" tasks from other workers that have more tasks than they can handle. This helps to balance the workload across all workers and can significantly improve the overall computation time, especially in situations where the workload is not evenly distributed.

- Prefetching: This strategy involves workers starting to fetch the data for a task before the task is ready to execute. This can help to hide the latency of data transfer, which can be a significant factor in distributed computations. By starting to fetch the data early, the worker can be ready to execute the task as soon as it becomes ready.

- Data Locality: The scheduler tries to assign tasks to workers in a way that minimizes data transfer between workers. For example, if a task depends on the result of another task that was executed on a particular worker, the scheduler will try to assign the task to the same worker. This can reduce the amount of data that needs to be transferred between workers, which can be a significant factor in distributed computations.

- Task Prioritization: The scheduler prioritizes tasks based on their dependencies. Tasks that are dependencies of many other tasks are given higher priority, as completing these tasks early can make more tasks ready to execute. This can help to reduce the overall computation time by ensuring that the tasks that are most critical to the progress of the computation are executed first.

- Dynamic Scheduling: The scheduler makes scheduling decisions on-the-fly as tasks are completed and new tasks become ready to execute. This allows the scheduler to adapt to the current state of the computation and make optimal scheduling decisions based on the most up-to-date information.

- Task Fusion: In some cases, the scheduler can "fuse" multiple tasks into a single task to reduce the overhead of task scheduling. This can be particularly beneficial for computations that involve many small tasks.

These strategies help Dask to optimize task scheduling and verify efficient execution of computations in a distributed system. They allow Dask to adapt to the current state of the computation, balance the workload across workers, minimize data transfer, prioritize critical tasks, and reduce scheduling overhead.

Implement Work Stealing

Work stealing is a strategy used by Dask's distributed scheduler to balance the workload across all workers in the cluster. When a worker finishes its tasks and becomes idle, it can "steal" tasks from other workers that are still busy. This helps to verify that all workers are utilized as much as possible, which can significantly improve the overall computation time.

In Dask, work stealing is enabled by default, and you don't need to do anything special to use it. The scheduler automatically uses work stealing whenever it is beneficial.

The given below is a practical illustration of how work stealing can improve the computation time:

```
from dask.distributed import Client
import dask.array as da

# Connect to the Dask distributed cluster
client = Client('<scheduler-address>')

# Create a large Dask array
x = da.random.random((10000, 10000), chunks=(1000, 1000))

# Define a function that performs a heavy computation
def heavy_computation(x):
    return x**2 + x**3
```

```
# Apply the function to the array
y = x.map_blocks(heavy_computation)

# Call compute to start the computation
result = y.compute()
```

In the above sample program, the map_blocks function applies the heavy_computation function to each block of the Dask array. Each application of the function is a separate task, and these tasks are distributed across the workers in the cluster. Without work stealing, some workers might finish their tasks early and become idle, while others are still busy. With work stealing, the idle workers can "steal" tasks from the busy workers, ensuring that all workers are utilized as much as possible.

You can monitor the work stealing in action by opening the Dask dashboard in your web browser and navigating to the "Task Stream" view. Here, you can see the progress of tasks as they are being executed by the workers. When work stealing occurs, you will see tasks being moved from one worker to another.

Run Prefetching

Prefetching is another strategy used by Dask's distributed scheduler to optimize task scheduling. The idea behind prefetching is to start fetching the data for a task before the task is ready to execute. This can help to hide the latency of data transfer, which can be a significant factor in distributed computations.

In Dask, prefetching is automatically handled by the scheduler. When a worker finishes a task and asks the scheduler for a new task to execute, the scheduler not only tells the worker which task to execute next, but also which tasks are likely to be executed in the near future. The worker can then start fetching the data for these future tasks in the background, while it is executing the current task. This means that by the time the worker is ready to execute a future task, the data for the task is already available, and the worker doesn't have to wait for the data to be transferred. This can significantly improve the overall computation time, especially in situations where data transfer is a bottleneck.

The given below is a practical illustration of how prefetching can improve the computation time:

```
from dask.distributed import Client
import dask.array as da
```

```python
# Connect to the Dask distributed cluster
client = Client('<scheduler-address>')

# Create a large Dask array
x = da.random.random((10000, 10000), chunks=(1000, 1000))

# Define a function that performs a heavy computation
def heavy_computation(x):
    return x**2 + x**3

# Apply the function to the array
y = x.map_blocks(heavy_computation)

# Call compute to start the computation
result = y.compute()
```

In the absence of prefetching, a worker has to pause and wait for the necessary data to arrive before it can begin processing a given task. However, with prefetching enabled, the worker can proactively start downloading the required data for an upcoming task while it is still busy with another task. This assures that the data is already available when the worker is set to begin the new task. To observe the impact of prefetching, you can access the Dask dashboard and go to the "Task Stream" section. This view allows you to monitor the real-time progress of tasks as they are carried out by the workers. Effective prefetching is indicated by reduced idle time for the workers, minimizing the time they spend waiting for data transfers.

Instrument Data Locality

Data locality is an important concept in distributed computing and is another strategy used by Dask's distributed scheduler to optimize task scheduling. The idea behind data locality is to minimize the amount of data that needs to be transferred between workers. This is done by scheduling tasks on the workers that already have the data they need to execute the tasks.

In Dask, the scheduler keeps track of where each piece of data is stored. When it needs to schedule a task, it tries to assign the task to a worker that already has the data the task needs. If multiple workers have the data, the scheduler chooses the worker that is least busy. If no worker has the data, the scheduler chooses the worker that is closest to the data in terms of network topology.

Following is a sample demonstration of how data locality can improve the computation time:

```python
from dask.distributed import Client
import dask.array as da

# Connect to the Dask distributed cluster
client = Client('<scheduler-address>')

# Create a large Dask array
x = da.random.random((10000, 10000), chunks=(1000, 1000))

# Define a function that performs a heavy computation
def heavy_computation(x):
    return x**2 + x**3

# Apply the function to the array
y = x.map_blocks(heavy_computation)

# Call compute to start the computation
result = y.compute()
```

When data locality is absent, a task may require data to be moved from one worker to another before it can run. In contrast, with data locality, the scheduler aims to allocate tasks to workers that already possess the necessary data, thereby reducing data transfer requirements. As said previously, you may observe the impact of data locality, you can access the Dask dashboard and go to the "Task Stream" section. This will display the real-time progress of tasks as they're processed by the workers. Effective data locality will result in fewer data transfers between workers, leading to a notable reduction in overall computation duration.

Implement Dynamic Scheduling

Dynamic scheduling is another strategy used by Dask's distributed scheduler to optimize task scheduling. The idea behind dynamic scheduling is to make scheduling decisions on-the-fly as tasks are completed and new tasks become ready to execute. This allows the scheduler to adapt to the current state of the computation and make optimal scheduling decisions based on the most up-to-date information.

In a static scheduling approach, the schedule of tasks is determined in advance and does not change during the computation. This can be efficient for computations where the workload is predictable and evenly distributed, but it can be less efficient for computations where the workload is unpredictable or unevenly distributed. In contrast, dynamic scheduling allows the scheduler to adapt to the workload as it evolves during the computation. For example, if a task takes longer to complete than expected, the scheduler can assign more tasks to other workers to balance the workload. Or if a worker becomes idle because it has finished its tasks, the scheduler can assign new tasks to it to keep it busy.

The given below is a practical illustration of how dynamic scheduling can improve the computation time:

```
from dask.distributed import Client
import dask.array as da

# Connect to the Dask distributed cluster
client = Client('<scheduler-address>')

# Create a large Dask array
x = da.random.random((10000, 10000), chunks=(1000, 1000))

# Define a function that performs a heavy computation
def heavy_computation(x):
    return x**2 + x**3

# Apply the function to the array
y = x.map_blocks(heavy_computation)

# Call compute to start the computation
result = y.compute()
```

In the absence of dynamic scheduling, the task sequence is pre-set and remains static throughout the computation process. On the other hand, dynamic scheduling allows the scheduler to continuously adjust the task lineup based on completed tasks and newly available tasks. This confirms optimal workload distribution and maximizes worker utilization. Effective dynamic scheduling minimizes worker idle time by promptly assigning new tasks as soon as current ones are completed.

Deploy Task Fusion

Task fusion, also known as task merging, is another optimization strategy used by Dask to enhance the efficiency of computations. The idea behind task fusion is to merge multiple tasks into a single task, thereby reducing the overhead associated with task scheduling and execution. In Dask, as said previously, each operation you perform on a Dask collection like a Dask array or a Dask dataframe creates a new task. When you chain multiple operations together, this can result in a large number of small tasks. Each task has an associated overhead, as the scheduler needs to decide when and where to run the task, and the worker needs to fetch the task's data, execute the task, and store the result.

By fusing multiple tasks into a single task, this overhead can be significantly reduced. The fused task performs all the operations of the original tasks in a single step, which can be much more efficient than performing the operations separately.

The given below is a practical illustration of how task fusion can improve the computation time:

```
from dask.distributed import Client
import dask.array as da

# Connect to the Dask distributed cluster
client = Client('<scheduler-address>')

# Create a large Dask array
x = da.random.random((10000, 10000), chunks=(1000, 1000))

# Chain multiple operations together
y = (x + 1) * 2 - 3

# Call compute to start the computation
result = y.compute()
```

In the above sample program, the operations x + 1, * 2, and - 3 are chained together. Without task fusion, each operation would create a new task, resulting in three tasks in total. With task fusion, the three operations are merged into a single task, which performs all three operations in a single step. You can monitor the effect of task fusion by opening the Dask dashboard in your web browser and navigating to the "Task Graph" view. Here, you can see the task graph for the computation, which shows how tasks are merged together. When task fusion is effective, you will see fewer tasks in the task graph, which can significantly improve the overall computation time.

Understanding Fault Tolerance

Fault tolerance is a critical aspect of any distributed system, including Dask. It refers to the system's ability to continue functioning correctly, even in the event of failures or errors within the system. In the context of Dask, fault tolerance confirms that your computations can continue and successfully complete even if some tasks fail or if some workers in your cluster become unavailable.

Dask's distributed scheduler is designed to be fault-tolerant. It keeps track of the state of all tasks and workers in the system. If a task fails, the scheduler can reschedule the task to be executed on a different worker. If a worker becomes unavailable, the scheduler can redistribute the worker's tasks to other workers in the cluster.

This fault tolerance is achieved through a combination of mechanisms:

- Task retries: If a task fails, the scheduler can automatically retry the task a certain number of times. This can be useful for handling transient errors, such as temporary network issues.

- Task replication: For critical tasks, the scheduler can replicate the task on multiple workers. This way, if one worker fails, another worker can continue the task.

- Worker heartbeats: Each worker periodically sends a "heartbeat" message to the scheduler to indicate that it is still alive. If the scheduler does not receive a heartbeat from a worker within a certain time period, it assumes that the worker has failed and redistributes its tasks to other workers.

- Resilient data storage: Dask can store intermediate results of computations in a resilient manner, for example, by replicating the data on multiple workers or by storing the data in a distributed file system. This confirms that the data is not lost if a worker fails.

The given below is a practical illustration of how Dask's fault tolerance can be beneficial:

```
from dask.distributed import Client, progress
import dask.array as da

# Connect to the Dask distributed cluster
client = Client('<scheduler-address>')
```

```
# Create a large Dask array
x = da.random.random((10000, 10000), chunks=(1000, 1000))

# Define a function that performs a heavy computation
def heavy_computation(x):
    return x**2 + x**3

# Apply the function to the array
y = x.map_blocks(heavy_computation)

# Call compute to start the computation
future = client.compute(y)

# Monitor the progress of the computation
progress(future)
```

In the above sample program, the compute function starts the computation and returns a Future object. The progress function can be used to monitor the progress of the computation. If a task fails or a worker becomes unavailable during the computation, Dask's fault tolerance mechanisms verify that the computation can continue and successfully complete, even in the face of failures or errors within the system.

Scaling Dask Clusters

Scaling is a fundamental aspect of distributed computing, and Dask is no exception. The need for scaling arises when the computational requirements exceed the capacity of a single machine. This could be due to the size of the data, the complexity of the computations, or both. Scaling allows you to leverage multiple machines to perform computations in parallel, thereby increasing the overall computational capacity.

Dask provides two main ways to scale your computations:

- Scaling up (also known as vertical scaling) involves increasing the computational resources of a single machine, such as adding more CPUs, more memory, or faster storage. Dask can take advantage of these additional resources to perform computations more quickly.

- Scaling out (also known as horizontal scaling) involves adding more machines to the cluster. Dask's distributed scheduler can distribute tasks across all the machines in the cluster, allowing computations to be performed in parallel.

Scaling a Dask cluster can be achieved programmatically using the Cluster object provided by Dask's distributed scheduler. Following is a sample demonstration:

```python
from dask.distributed import Client, LocalCluster

# Create a local Dask cluster
cluster = LocalCluster()

# Connect to the cluster
client = Client(cluster)

# Print the current number of workers
print(f'Current number of workers: {len(cluster.workers)}')

# Scale up the cluster by adding more workers
cluster.scale(10)

# Print the new number of workers
print(f'New number of workers: {len(cluster.workers)}')

# Perform a computation
result = client.submit(lambda x: x**2, 10).result()
print(f'Result: {result}')

# Scale down the cluster by removing workers
cluster.scale(2)

# Print the final number of workers
print(f'Final number of workers: {len(cluster.workers)}')
```

In the above sample program, the LocalCluster object represents a Dask cluster running on the local machine. The scale method is used to change the number of workers in the cluster. The

Client object is used to submit computations to the cluster and retrieve the results. This example demonstrates how to scale a Dask cluster programmatically. However, in a real-world scenario, you would typically use a cluster manager (like Kubernetes, YARN, or Mesos) to manage the scaling of your Dask cluster.

Resource Usage and Management

Resource management is a critical aspect of distributed computing. It involves efficiently allocating and managing computational resources such as CPU, memory, disk space, and network bandwidth among the tasks in a distributed system. In Dask, resource management is primarily handled by the distributed scheduler, which schedules tasks based on their resource requirements and the available resources on the workers.

Resource usage can become a concern in several circumstances:

- If your computations involve large datasets that do not fit into memory, you may run into out-of-memory errors. Dask mitigates this issue by using lazy evaluation and chunking large datasets into smaller pieces that fit into memory. However, you still need to verify that your workers have enough memory to handle the largest chunk.

- If your computations are CPU-intensive, you may max out the CPU usage on your workers. This can slow down other tasks and lead to longer computation times. Dask's scheduler tries to balance the load across all workers to prevent any single worker from becoming a bottleneck.

- In a distributed system, data needs to be transferred between workers. If your computations involve a lot of data transfer, this can consume a significant amount of network bandwidth and slow down your computations. Dask's scheduler uses several strategies to minimize data transfer, such as scheduling tasks on the worker that already has the necessary data and replicating frequently used data across multiple workers.

- If your computations generate a lot of intermediate results that are stored on disk, you may run out of disk space. Dask provides options to control the storage of intermediate results, such as spilling to disk only when memory is full.

To manage resources effectively, you can use several tools and technologies in conjunction with Dask:

- Tools like Kubernetes, YARN, and Mesos can automatically scale your Dask cluster based on the current workload. They can add or remove workers as needed, ensuring that your cluster always has the right amount of resources.

- Dask provides a web-based dashboard that gives you real-time insights into the resource usage of your cluster. You can see how much CPU, memory, and network bandwidth is being used by each worker and each task. This can help you identify bottlenecks and optimize your computations.

- Dask allows you to specify resource quotas for tasks. For example, you can specify that a task requires a certain amount of memory or a certain number of CPU cores. The scheduler will take these quotas into account when scheduling the task.

- Dask's scheduler tries to schedule tasks on the worker that already has the necessary data. This reduces the amount of data that needs to be transferred over the network, saving network bandwidth and reducing computation times.

To sum up, resource management is a crucial aspect of distributed computing with Dask. By understanding the resource requirements of your computations and using the right tools and strategies, you can confirm that your Dask cluster uses resources efficiently and performs computations as quickly as possible.

Summary

In this chapter, we kicked off our exploration by dissecting the architecture of Dask's Distributed Scheduler, the linchpin of its distributed capabilities. This scheduler orchestrates the execution of tasks across a multitude of workers, optimizing resource utilization in the process.

Next, we transitioned into the hands-on aspects of operating a Dask Distributed Cluster. From setting up and initiating a Dask cluster to monitoring its real-time performance via Dask's intuitive dashboard, we covered it all. Additionally, we examined the scalability of Dask clusters, learning how to expand their capacity by either augmenting the number of workers (horizontal scaling) or boosting the resources allocated to each worker (vertical scaling).

Our journey also took us deep into the mechanics of task scheduling within distributed environments. We gained insights into several optimization strategies, including work stealing, prefetching, data locality, dynamic scheduling, and task fusion. Alongside, we explored Dask's robust fault-tolerance mechanisms that safeguard ongoing computations against task failures or worker downtimes. To round off the chapter, we delved into the critical subject of resource management, highlighting potential challenges and how Dask, in conjunction with other technologies, offers effective solutions.

Chapter 5: Advanced Dask: APIs and Building Blocks

Introduction to Algorithms

In the journey so far, we have explored the fundamentals of Dask, its architecture, and its application in parallel and distributed computing. We've learned about Dask's collections like arrays, dataframes, and bags, and how they enable us to work with large datasets that don't fit into memory. We've also delved into Dask's computation model, including lazy evaluation and task graphs. We've seen how Dask's distributed scheduler enables us to scale our computations across multiple machines, and we've learned about various strategies for optimizing task scheduling and resource management in distributed systems.

We shall turn our attention to algorithms and how we can work with them in Dask. Algorithms form the backbone of any computational task. They define the steps that the computer needs to follow to solve a particular problem. Dask provides a high-level interface for defining and executing these algorithms. At its core, Dask uses a directed acyclic graph (DAG) to represent the computations. Each node in the graph represents a task, and the edges represent the dependencies between tasks. This graph-based representation allows Dask to execute tasks in parallel whenever possible, and to distribute tasks across multiple workers in a distributed system.

When working with algorithms in Dask, there are a few key concepts to keep in mind such as chunking, lazy evaluation, task fusion, and parallel algorithms. In the following sections, we will explore these concepts in more detail and see how they can be applied to solve real-world problems using Dask.

Custom Algorithms?

Creating custom algorithms in Dask is essential when you need to perform complex computations that cannot be easily expressed using Dask's high-level APIs. Dask provides the delayed function, which allows you to write your own algorithms that can be parallelized and executed on a Dask cluster.

The delayed function works by wrapping your Python functions and delaying their execution. Instead of executing the function immediately, Dask adds the function to the computation graph and executes it later when you call compute(). This allows Dask to optimize the computation and execute it in parallel.

The given below is a practical illustration of how you can create a custom algorithm using delayed:

```
from dask import delayed

# Define a Python function
def increment(x):
```

```python
    return x + 1

# Wrap the function with delayed
increment = delayed(increment)

# Now you can use the function in a Dask computation
x = increment(1)
y = increment(x)
result = y.compute()
```

In the above sample program, the increment function is executed in a delayed manner. Dask builds a computation graph that includes two increment tasks, and then executes the tasks in parallel when compute() is called. You can also use delayed to create more complex algorithms. For example, following is how you can implement a simple map-reduce algorithm using delayed:

```python
from dask import delayed

# Define a Python function for the map phase
def increment(x):
    return x + 1

# Define a Python function for the reduce phase
def add(x, y):
    return x + y

# Wrap the functions with delayed
increment = delayed(increment)
add = delayed(add)

# Create a Dask array
import dask.array as da
x = da.ones((10000,), chunks=(1000,))

# Perform the map phase
```

```
y = [increment(xi) for xi in x]

# Perform the reduce phase
result = add(*y)

# Compute the result
result = result.compute()
```

In the above sample program, the increment function is applied to each chunk of the Dask array in the map phase, and the add function is used to combine the results in the reduce phase. The computation is executed in parallel when compute() is called. Creating custom algorithms with Dask gives you the flexibility to express complex computations that cannot be easily expressed using Dask's high-level APIs. However, it also requires a deeper understanding of Dask's computation model and how to optimize computations for parallel execution.

Exploring Dask Joblib

Dask integrates with the popular Joblib library to provide an effective solution for parallel and distributed computing. Joblib is a Python library that provides support for parallel and distributed computing, and it's often used in scientific Python environments. It's particularly well-suited for tasks that involve heavy use of numpy arrays. Joblib provides a simple way to parallelize for-loops, which is a common pattern in scientific computing. However, Joblib's built-in parallel backends, which include threading and multiprocessing, are not always the most efficient choice for large-scale computations. This is where Dask comes in.

Dask provides a Joblib backend that allows you to use Dask's distributed scheduler for Joblib computations. This means that you can use Dask to execute Joblib computations on a cluster of machines, rather than just a single machine. This can lead to significant speedups for large computations. The Dask Joblib backend also integrates with Dask's other features, such as its dynamic task scheduling and its ability to work with larger-than-memory datasets. This makes it a powerful tool for parallel and distributed computing.

The given below is a practical illustration of how you can use the Dask Joblib backend:

```
from sklearn.datasets import load_digits
from sklearn.model_selection import RandomizedSearchCV
from sklearn.svm import SVC
import joblib
```

```python
from dask.distributed import Client

# Start a Dask client
client = Client()

# Load some data
digits = load_digits()

# Define a parameter search
param_space = {
    'C': np.logspace(-6, 6, 13),
    'gamma': np.logspace(-8, 8, 17),
    'tol': np.logspace(-4, -1, 4),
    'class_weight': [None, 'balanced'],
}

model = SVC(kernel='rbf')
search = RandomizedSearchCV(model, param_space, cv=3, n_iter=50, verbose=10)

# Use Dask to perform the parameter search
with joblib.parallel_backend('dask'):
    search.fit(digits.data, digits.target)
```

In the above sample program, a parameter search is performed on a support vector machine (SVM) model using the Dask Joblib backend. The RandomizedSearchCV function from Scikit-learn is used to perform the parameter search, and the computation is parallelized using Dask.

Parallelizing Code using Joblib

We shall now dive deeper into another illustrative example that demonstrates the power of integrating Dask with Joblib for parallelizing computational tasks. Specifically, you can employ a straightforward function designed to mimic a computational process. This function will simulate the time-consuming nature of real-world computations by incorporating a sleep function that pauses execution for a random duration.

To kick things off, we shall start by crafting the function that will serve as the cornerstone of our example:

```
import time
import random

def slow_function(i):
    print(f"Task {i} started")
    time.sleep(random.random())
    print(f"Task {i} finished")
    return i
```

This function simulates a task that takes a variable amount of time to complete. It prints a message when it starts and finishes, and then returns its input argument.

Next, you can use Joblib to parallelize this function:

```
from joblib import Parallel, delayed
from dask.distributed import Client

# Start a Dask client
client = Client()

# Create a list of tasks
tasks = [delayed(slow_function)(i) for i in range(10)]

# Use Dask to execute the tasks in parallel
with joblib.parallel_backend('dask'):
    results = Parallel()(tasks)
```

In this code, we first create a Dask client, which connects to the Dask scheduler and allows us to execute computations. We then create a list of tasks using the delayed function, which tells Dask to delay the execution of the function until we call compute(). We then use the Parallel function from Joblib to execute the tasks in parallel. The parallel_backend('dask') context manager tells Joblib to use Dask as the backend for parallel execution. When you run this code, you should see the tasks being executed in parallel, with the start and finish messages being printed out of order due to the parallel execution.

This example serves as a comprehensive walkthrough on how to leverage the power of Dask in conjunction with Joblib to achieve parallelized computations. The cornerstone of this approach is the 'delayed' function, a versatile utility provided by Dask. This function enables you to construct intricate computational tasks using standard Python syntax, essentially allowing you to write code as you normally would, without worrying about parallelization at that moment. Once you've built up these complex computations, you can then unleash the full potential of Dask's distributed scheduler to execute them. The scheduler takes care of distributing the tasks across multiple workers, ensuring that they are executed in parallel, thereby optimizing the computational efficiency. This is a perfect example of how Dask's capabilities can be extended and integrated with other libraries to achieve high-performance computing in Python.

Understanding Numba

Numba is an open-source Just-In-Time (JIT) compiler that translates a subset of Python and NumPy code into fast machine code. It uses the LLVM compiler infrastructure to compile Python syntax into machine code that is designed to run at native machine code speed. Numba is primarily used to speed up numerical computations and data-heavy Python applications. It's particularly effective for functions that perform heavy computations on arrays, such as functions that are written in a vectorized style, similar to how you would write code for NumPy.

The primary feature of Numba is its ability to dynamically compile Python functions, not whole applications, and especially compute-intensive functions operating on large arrays. For this, Numba provides a simple interface through a set of decorators that can be applied to your functions to instruct Numba to compile them.

Given below is a simple example of using Numba:

```python
from numba import jit
import numpy as np

@jit(nopython=True)
def sum2d(arr):
    M, N = arr.shape
    result = 0.0
    for i in range(M):
        for j in range(N):
            result += arr[i,j]
    return result
```

```python
a = np.arange(1.0, 10000000.0).reshape(1000, 10000)
print(sum2d(a))
```

In the above sample program, the @jit(nopython=True) decorator tells Numba to compile the sum2d function in "nopython" mode, which yields the best performance. The function then performs a simple 2D sum over a NumPy array.

Numba is also capable of generating compiled code for a wide range of hardware, including CPUs, GPUs, and other accelerators. This makes it a powerful tool for high-performance computing. Numba is not a replacement for Python but a tool that works best when used for functions performing heavy computations. It's not suited for all Python code, especially code that is I/O heavy, or that heavily uses Python data structures like lists and dictionaries. Numba is best used with NumPy arrays, functions that are compute heavy, and that would benefit from being run on a variety of hardware.

Integrate Dask with Numba

Dask and Numba can be used together to achieve high performance in Python, especially for numerical computations. Dask can handle parallelism and larger-than-memory computations, while Numba can speed up CPU-bound tasks. Following is a step-wise walkthrough on how to use Dask and Numba together.

Define Function with Numba

First, we define a function that performs some heavy computation. We then use the @jit decorator from Numba to compile this function. This will speed up the execution of the function when it's called.

```python
from numba import jit
import numpy as np

@jit(nopython=True)
def heavy_computation(x, y):
    return np.sqrt(x**2 + y**2)
```

In the above sample program, the heavy_computation function computes the Euclidean distance between two points x and y. The @jit(nopython=True) decorator tells Numba to compile this function in "nopython" mode, which yields the best performance.

Create Dask Arrays

Next, we create two Dask arrays that you can use as input for our function. Dask arrays are similar to NumPy arrays, but they can be larger than memory and their computations can be parallelized.

```
import dask.array as da

x = da.random.random((10000, 10000), chunks=(1000, 1000))
y = da.random.random((10000, 10000), chunks=(1000, 1000))
```

In the above sample program, x and y are Dask arrays with shape (10000, 10000). The chunks argument specifies the chunk size, which determines how the arrays are divided into smaller pieces for parallel computation.

Apply Function to Dask Arrays

We can apply our Numba-compiled function to the Dask arrays using the da.map_blocks function. This function applies a function to each chunk of a Dask array.

```
result = da.map_blocks(heavy_computation, x, y)
```

In the above sample program, da.map_blocks(heavy_computation, x, y) applies the heavy_computation function to each chunk of x and y.

Compute the Result

Finally, we can compute the result using the compute method. This triggers the actual computation.

```
result = result.compute()
```

In the above sample program, result.compute() triggers the computation and returns the result as a NumPy array. This fusion of Dask's distributed computing and Numba's Just-In-Time (JIT) compilation creates a robust platform for tackling complex computational challenges. Together, they offer a comprehensive solution for both data scalability and computational speed, setting a new standard for high-performance computing in Python.

Understanding NumPy

NumPy, short for Numerical Python, is a fundamental package for scientific computing in

Python. It provides a high-performance, multidimensional array object and tools for working with these arrays. NumPy is the foundation upon which many other scientific processing libraries are built, including Pandas, SciPy, and Matplotlib. The core functionality of NumPy is its ndarray (n-dimensional array) object, which is a fast, flexible container for large datasets in Python. Arrays enable you to perform mathematical operations on whole blocks of data using similar syntax to the equivalent operations between scalar elements.

The given below is a simple example of using NumPy:

```
import numpy as np

# Create a NumPy array
a = np.array([1, 2, 3, 4, 5])

# Perform operations on the array
print(a + 10)
print(a * 2)
```

In the above sample program, a is a NumPy array. We can perform operations like addition and multiplication on the entire array at once, which is much more efficient than doing it element by element.

NumPy is particularly useful for numerical computations because it provides efficient operations on arrays, including mathematical, logical, shape manipulation, sorting, selecting, I/O, discrete Fourier transforms, basic linear algebra, basic statistical operations, random simulation and much more. While NumPy provides the computational foundation for these operations, it's often used in conjunction with other libraries that provide higher-level abstractions and flexible data manipulation. For example, Pandas provides flexible data structures for manipulating structured data, SciPy extends NumPy with more advanced algorithms, and Matplotlib provides powerful data visualization capabilities.

Numba, on the other hand, is a just-in-time compiler for Python that's best used for functions that perform heavy computations. While Numba does optimize some NumPy operations, it's not a replacement for NumPy. Instead, Numba can be used to speed up your existing NumPy-based code without having to switch to a lower-level language like C or Fortran.

Integrate Dask with NumPy

Integrating Dask with NumPy is straightforward because Dask was designed to be compatible with NumPy. Dask arrays are chunked into many small NumPy arrays, allowing you to work with larger-than-memory datasets using a familiar NumPy-like API. Following is a step-wise walkthrough on how to use Dask and NumPy together.

Import Dask and NumPy

First, we need to import the necessary libraries.

```
import numpy as np
import dask.array as da
```

Create Large NumPy Array

Next, we shall create a large NumPy array. For this example, you can create an array of one billion (1e9) elements.

```
size = int(1e9)
x_np = np.random.random(size)
```

Convert NumPy Array to Dask Array

We can convert the NumPy array to a Dask array using the from_array function. You can also specify a chunk size.

```
chunk_size = int(1e6)
x_da = da.from_array(x_np, chunks=chunk_size)
```

In the above sample program, x_da is a Dask array that's chunked into smaller NumPy arrays of size 1e6.

Perform Operations on Dask Array

We can now perform operations on the Dask array just like we would with a NumPy array. However, these operations are lazy; they build up a computation graph, but the actual computations aren't performed yet.

```
y_da = x_da + 1
z_da = da.exp(y_da)
```

In the above sample program, y_da is the result of adding 1 to each element in x_da, and z_da is the result of applying the exponential function to each element in y_da.

Compute Result

Finally, we can compute the result using the compute method. This triggers the actual computations.

```
z_np = z_da.compute()
```

In the above sample program, z_da.compute() triggers the computation and returns the result as a NumPy array. Utilizing Dask alongside NumPy opens up a realm of possibilities for handling datasets that exceed the limitations of your machine's memory. What makes this combination particularly compelling is that Dask offers an API that closely mimics the NumPy interface. This means you can continue to work in the familiar NumPy-like environment you're accustomed to, but with the added advantage of being able to manage much larger datasets.

Exploring Xarray

Xarray is a Python package that makes working with labeled multi-dimensional arrays simple, efficient, and fun! Xarray introduces labels in the form of dimensions, coordinates and attributes on top of raw NumPy-like arrays, which allows for a more intuitive, more concise, and less error-prone developer experience. The package includes a large and growing library of domain-agnostic functions for advanced analytics and visualization with these data structures.

Xarray is inspired by and borrows heavily from pandas, the popular data manipulation package focused on labeled tabular data. It is particularly tailored to working with netCDF files, which were the source of Xarray's data model, and integrates tightly with dask for parallel computing.

The given below is a simple example of using Xarray:

```
import xarray as xr
import numpy as np

# Create some sample data
data = np.random.rand(4, 3, 2)

# Wrap the data in an Xarray Dataset
ds = xr.Dataset(
    {
```

```
    "temperature": (("x", "y", "time"), data),
  },
  coords={
    "x": [10, 20, 30, 40],
    "y": [150, 120],
    "time": pd.date_range("2023-08-01", periods=3),
    "reference_time": pd.Timestamp("2023-08-01"),
  },
)

print(ds)
```

In the above sample program, ds is an Xarray Dataset that contains one variable (temperature) and three dimensions (x, y, time). Each dimension has a label (e.g., x is labeled with [10, 20, 30, 40]), and there's also a reference_time coordinate.

Xarray's labeled dimensions free us from having to track the order of dimensions and allow us to focus on operations that make sense with our data, regardless of its shape. This makes our code more readable and less prone to bugs. While pandas excels at working with tabular data, Xarray is better suited for working with multi-dimensional arrays. For example, if you're working with data that has more than two dimensions, such as climate or weather data, images, or other similar datasets, Xarray will often be easier and more intuitive to use than pandas.

Integrate Dask with Xarray

Dask and Xarray integrate smoothly, and Xarray Datasets can be parallelized using Dask for out-of-core, scalable computations. Following is a step-wise walkthrough on how to use Dask and Xarray together.

Import Dask, Xarray, and NumPy

First, we need to import the necessary libraries.

```
import numpy as np
import xarray as xr
import dask.array as da
```

Create Large Dask Array

Next, we shall create a large Dask array. For this example, you can create an array of one billion (1e9) elements, chunked into smaller arrays of one million (1e6) elements each.

```
size = int(1e9)
chunk_size = int(1e6)
x_da = da.random.random(size, chunks=chunk_size)
```

Convert Dask Array to Xarray DataArray

We can convert the Dask array to an Xarray DataArray. You can also add some labels to the data.

```
x_xr = xr.DataArray(x_da, dims='x', coords={'x': np.arange(size)})
```

In the above sample program, x_xr is an Xarray DataArray that wraps the Dask array x_da. The 'x' dimension is labelled with a range from 0 to size.

Perform Operations on Xarray DataArray

We can now perform operations on the Xarray DataArray just like we would with a NumPy array. However, these operations are lazy; they build up a computation graph, but the actual computations aren't performed yet.

```
y_xr = x_xr + 1
z_xr = np.exp(y_xr)
```

In the above sample program, y_xr is the result of adding 1 to each element in x_xr, and z_xr is the result of applying the exponential function to each element in y_xr.

Compute Result

Finally, we can compute the result using the compute method. This triggers the actual computations.

```
z_np = z_xr.compute()
```

In this illustrative example, invoking z_xr.compute() serves as the catalyst that initiates the actual computation, culminating in the output being returned as a NumPy array. The beauty of integrating Dask with Xarray lies in the ability to handle datasets that exceed the available memory, all while utilizing an API that closely resembles that of NumPy. This not only makes the transition smoother for those familiar with NumPy but also opens the door to the advantages of parallel and distributed computing. Moreover, Xarray brings its own set of unique features to the table, most notably its labeled data structures. These labels significantly enhance code readability by providing a more intuitive way to interact with multi-dimensional arrays.

Summary

In this comprehensive chapter, we embarked on an in-depth journey into the realm of algorithms, specifically focusing on how they can be effectively implemented using Dask. The chapter kicked off with a succinct recapitulation of key takeaways from previous chapters, setting the stage for a deeper dive into a plethora of Dask-specific concepts. These included Dask arrays, dataframes, bags, and the intriguing notion of delayed computations. Each of these concepts was meticulously unpacked, accompanied by hands-on examples to reinforce the theoretical understanding and provide a practical context.

Following this foundational groundwork, we transitioned into the fascinating subject of crafting custom algorithms within the Dask ecosystem. This segment was especially enlightening because it showcased the remarkable flexibility and computational prowess that Dask offers. We delved into the nuances of integrating Dask with Joblib, a feature that simplifies the parallelization of code, thereby making it more efficient. This was complemented by an exhaustive discourse on Dask's low-level primitives, elucidating how these building blocks can be harnessed to architect more intricate and resource-efficient algorithms.

As we ventured into the concluding sections of the chapter, we were introduced to a suite of auxiliary tools that can be synergistically used alongside Dask. These included Numba for just-in-time compilation, NumPy for numerical operations, and Xarray for labeled multi-dimensional arrays. Each of these tools was dissected in great detail, complete with practical examples that demonstrated their seamless integration with Dask for optimized computational tasks. In addition, we touched upon the critical aspect of resource management in distributed computing environments, elaborating on how Dask's capabilities can be leveraged to manage resources effectively. Finally, the chapter wrapped up with an insightful learnings on the mechanisms of fault tolerance within Dask, emphasizing its vital role in ensuring the reliability and robustness of parallel computing endeavors.

Chapter 6: Integrated Libraries: Dask with Pandas

Pandas Overview

Pandas is a popular data manipulation library in Python, known for its powerful data structures and data analysis tools. It provides two primary data structures - DataFrame and Series - that are used for manipulating different types of data. These data structures are flexible, efficient, and intuitive, making Pandas a go-to library for data analysis tasks. However, despite its many strengths, Pandas has some limitations when it comes to parallel processing. The primary limitation is that Pandas is not designed to work with datasets that don't fit into memory. This is a significant constraint when working with large datasets, as it's not uncommon for data scientists to work with gigabytes or even terabytes of data.

Another limitation of Pandas is that it doesn't inherently support parallel processing. This means that when you execute a Pandas operation, it runs on a single core and doesn't take advantage of the multiple cores that modern computers have. This can lead to inefficient use of computational resources and longer processing times. This is where Dask comes into play. Dask is a parallel computing library that integrates seamlessly with Pandas. It allows you to work with larger-than-memory datasets and can parallelize operations for better performance. Dask provides a Dask DataFrame, which is a large parallel DataFrame composed of smaller Pandas DataFrames, split along the index.

Dask DataFrames mimic Pandas DataFrames, which means you can write familiar syntax that looks much like regular Pandas code. The difference is that Dask operations are lazy; they build up a task graph to execute when you call compute(). This allows Dask to optimize the computation and execute it in parallel.

In the following sections, we will explore how to use Dask with Pandas to perform parallel processing of Pandas operations. We will cover various topics, including creating Dask DataFrames, performing operations on Dask DataFrames, and optimizing Dask computations. We will also learn how to handle larger-than-memory datasets with Dask and Pandas.

Creating Dask DataFrame

Creating a Dask DataFrame is similar to creating a Pandas DataFrame. You can create a Dask DataFrame from various data sources like CSV, SQL databases, or even from a Pandas DataFrame.

Given below is a quick example:

```
import dask.dataframe as dd
import pandas as pd
```

```
# Create a pandas dataframe
pdf = pd.DataFrame({
    'x': range(1000),
    'y': range(1000, 2000)
})

# Convert the pandas dataframe to a dask dataframe
ddf = dd.from_pandas(pdf, npartitions=4)
```

In the above example, we first create a Pandas DataFrame and then convert it into a Dask DataFrame using the dd.from_pandas() function. The npartitions parameter specifies the number of partitions to divide the data into.

We shall move on to handling missing data. Missing data is a common issue in real-world datasets. Both Pandas and Dask provide several methods for handling missing data, such as dropping the missing values or filling them with a specified value or a computed value (like mean, median, etc.).

The given below is a practical illustration of how you can handle missing data in a Dask DataFrame:

```
# Assume 'ddf' is a Dask DataFrame with some missing values

# To drop the rows with missing values
ddf = ddf.dropna()

# To fill the missing values with a specified value, say 0
ddf = ddf.fillna(0)

# To fill the missing values with mean of the non-missing values
ddf = ddf.fillna(ddf.mean().compute())
```

In the above example, dropna() function is used to drop the rows with missing values. The fillna() function is used to fill the missing values with a specified value or a computed value. Do verify that when filling with the mean of the non-missing values, we need to compute the mean first before passing it to fillna(), as Dask operations are lazy by nature.

Group Operations with Dask and Pandas

Group operations are a common task in data analysis. They involve splitting the data into groups based on some criteria, applying a function to each group independently, and then combining the results. This is often referred to as the split-apply-combine strategy.

In Pandas, we use the groupby() function to perform group operations. Dask DataFrames mimic this functionality, allowing you to perform group operations in a similar manner. However, the computation is lazily evaluated and performed in parallel.

The given below is a practical illustration of how you can perform group operations with Dask:

```
import dask.dataframe as dd
import pandas as pd

# Create a pandas dataframe
pdf = pd.DataFrame({
    'A': ['foo', 'bar', 'foo', 'bar', 'foo', 'bar', 'foo', 'foo'],
    'B': ['one', 'one', 'two', 'three', 'two', 'two', 'one', 'three'],
    'C': range(8),
    'D': range(10, 18)
})

# Convert the pandas dataframe to a dask dataframe
ddf = dd.from_pandas(pdf, npartitions=2)

# Perform a group operation
result = ddf.groupby('A').sum().compute()

print(result)
```

In the above example, we first create a Pandas DataFrame and then convert it into a Dask DataFrame. We then perform a group operation using the groupby() function. We group the data by column 'A' and calculate the sum of the other columns for each group. The compute() function is used to execute the computation. The result is a new DataFrame with the sum of columns 'C' and 'D' for each group in column 'A'.

Executing Joint Operations

Join operations are used to combine rows from two or more tables based on a related column between them. In Pandas, we use the merge() function to perform join operations. Dask DataFrames mimic this functionality, allowing you to perform join operations in a similar manner. However, the computation is lazily evaluated and performed in parallel.

The given below is a practical illustration of how you can perform join operations with Dask:

```
import dask.dataframe as dd
import pandas as pd

# Create two pandas dataframes
pdf1 = pd.DataFrame({
    'A': ['foo', 'bar', 'foo', 'bar', 'foo', 'bar', 'foo', 'foo'],
    'B': ['one', 'one', 'two', 'three', 'two', 'two', 'one', 'three'],
    'C': range(8),
})

pdf2 = pd.DataFrame({
    'A': ['foo', 'bar', 'foo', 'bar', 'foo', 'bar', 'foo', 'foo'],
    'B': ['one', 'one', 'two', 'three', 'two', 'two', 'one', 'three'],
    'D': range(10, 18)
})

# Convert the pandas dataframes to dask dataframes
ddf1 = dd.from_pandas(pdf1, npartitions=2)
ddf2 = dd.from_pandas(pdf2, npartitions=2)

# Perform a join operation
result = ddf1.merge(ddf2, on=['A', 'B']).compute()

print(result)
```

In the above example, we first create two Pandas DataFrames and then convert them into Dask DataFrames. We then perform a join operation using the merge() function. We join the dataframes on columns 'A' and 'B'. The compute() function is used to execute the computation. The result is a new DataFrame that combines the rows from the two dataframes based on the values in columns 'A' and 'B'.

Performing Time-series Analysis

Time-series analysis is a specialized form of statistical analysis that focuses on data that is ordered in a chronological sequence. This type of data, known as time-series data, is characterized by its temporal ordering, meaning that each data point is associated with a specific point in time. The analysis of such data involves various techniques aimed at understanding underlying patterns, trends, and anomalies over time. Dask, a powerful library for parallel computing in Python, offers support for time-series analysis through a subset of the Pandas time-series API.

In the realm of time-series analysis, Dask provides a robust set of tools that allow for efficient manipulation and querying of time-ordered data. Whether you're dealing with financial market data, sensor readings, or social media metrics, Dask's capabilities can be leveraged to perform complex calculations and transformations on large datasets. Its compatibility with a subset of Pandas' time-series API means that you can perform tasks like resampling, time-zone conversion, and rolling window calculations with ease.

The given below is a practical illustration of how you can perform time series analysis with Dask:

```
import dask.dataframe as dd
import pandas as pd

# Create a pandas dataframe with time series data
pdf = pd.DataFrame({
    'date': pd.date_range(start='1/1/2020', periods=100),
    'value': range(100)
})

# Convert the pandas dataframe to a dask dataframe
ddf = dd.from_pandas(pdf, npartitions=2)

# Set 'date' as the index (this will improve performance for subsequent operations)
ddf = ddf.set_index('date')

# Resample the data to calculate the monthly average
```

```
monthly_average = ddf.resample('M').mean().compute()

print(monthly_average)
```

In the above example, we first create a Pandas DataFrame with time series data and then convert it into a Dask DataFrame. We then set 'date' as the index, which will improve performance for subsequent operations. We then resample the data to calculate the monthly average using the resample() function. The compute() function is used to execute the computation. The result is a new DataFrame that contains the monthly average of the 'value' column.

Performance Analysis of Dask and Pandas

Dask and Pandas are both powerful tools for data analysis in Python, but they serve different purposes and are better suited to different types of tasks. Pandas is a software library for data manipulation and analysis. It provides data structures and functions needed to manipulate structured data, including functions for reading and writing data in a variety of formats. It's particularly good for interactive data exploration and using data manipulation methods like filtering, grouping, and merging data. Pandas is also great for tasks that require complex computations on smaller datasets that can fit in memory.

However, when it comes to larger datasets that don't fit into memory, this is where Dask shines. Dask is a parallel computing library that scales the existing Python ecosystem. This library coordinates with Python's existing scientific software stack to process large data while paralleling and distributing computations. Dask provides advanced parallelism for analytics, enabling performance at scale for the tools you love like Pandas, Numpy, and Scikit-Learn.

Dask DataFrames are a large parallel DataFrame composed of smaller Pandas DataFrames, split along the index. These Pandas DataFrames may live on disk for larger-than-memory computing on a single machine, or on many different machines in a cluster. One Dask DataFrame operation triggers many operations on the constituent Pandas DataFrames, allowing Dask to take advantage of available computational resources to execute operations in parallel.

When comparing performance, Dask DataFrames perform quite well against Pandas DataFrames, as long as you're working with larger datasets that don't fit into memory. For smaller datasets, the overhead of Dask's parallel computations can actually make it slower than Pandas. However, Dask's ability to handle larger-than-memory datasets and to use all the cores of your CPU can make it much faster than Pandas for larger datasets. In terms of functionality, Dask DataFrames implement a large subset of the Pandas API, but not all of it. This means that for some tasks, you might find that you need to use Pandas because Dask does not support the specific function you need. However, Dask is continually being developed and more and more of the Pandas API is being implemented.

The choice between Dask and Pandas will depend on the size of your dataset and the computations you need to perform. If you're working with smaller datasets and doing exploratory data analysis, Pandas is likely the best tool for the job. If you're working with larger datasets or need to perform complex computations that can be parallelized, Dask is a powerful tool that can significantly speed up your computations.

Summary

In this chapter, the focus was on the seamless integration of Dask with Pandas, a widely-used Python library for data manipulation and analysis. We discovered that Pandas excels in handling smaller datasets that can be accommodated in a computer's memory. However, when it comes to managing larger datasets that exceed memory limitations, Dask becomes the tool of choice. Dask DataFrames serve as large, parallelized DataFrames that are essentially composed of smaller Pandas DataFrames, enabling us to work with data that is too large to fit into memory.

We delved into a variety of operations that can be performed using Dask and Pandas in tandem. These included techniques for managing missing data, executing complex group and join operations, and conducting time-series analyses. Each operation was elucidated through practical examples, offering a hands-on approach to understanding the synergies between Dask and Pandas. Additionally, we examined the critical role of data partitioning in Dask, exploring how it significantly influences computational performance.

Towards the end of the chapter, we engaged in a performance evaluation, comparing Dask and Pandas. We found that Dask's ability to perform parallel computations gives it a speed advantage for larger datasets. However, it's worth noting that the computational overhead associated with parallel processing can make Dask less efficient than Pandas for smaller datasets. Therefore, the decision to use Dask or Pandas is contingent upon the dataset size and the specific computational requirements. This chapter served as a comprehensive walkthrough, equipping you with the knowledge to harness the capabilities of both Dask and Pandas for more effective data analysis.

Chapter 7: Integrated Libraries: Dask with Scikit-learn

Scikit-learn Overview

Scikit-learn is a popular machine learning library in Python that provides simple and efficient tools for data analysis and modeling. It includes a wide variety of algorithms for classification, regression, clustering, dimensionality reduction, and more. Scikit-learn's user-friendly API and extensive documentation have made it a go-to library for both beginners and experienced data scientists. However, when it comes to parallelizing scikit-learn models, several challenges arise. Parallelization refers to the process of dividing a task into sub-tasks that can be processed simultaneously, typically on multiple processors or cores.

While this can significantly speed up computations, it also introduces complexity and potential issues.

- Memory Constraints: Scikit-learn models can become quite large, especially when dealing with large datasets. Parallelizing these models means duplicating some of the data across multiple processors, which can lead to memory constraints.

- Communication Overhead: When parallelizing, the processors need to communicate with each other to share data and results. This communication can introduce overhead, slowing down the computation. The overhead can be particularly problematic when the communication needs to happen across different machines in a cluster.

- Load Balancing: Achieving optimal performance requires balancing the load across the processors evenly. If one processor finishes its task much earlier than others, it will sit idle, wasting resources. On the other hand, if one processor has much more work than others, it will become a bottleneck. Achieving this balance can be complex.

- Non-Thread-Safe Operations: Some operations in scikit-learn are not thread-safe, meaning they can't be safely executed in parallel threads. This can lead to unexpected behavior and bugs when attempting to parallelize certain parts of the computation.

- Algorithm Complexity: Not all algorithms can be easily parallelized. Some algorithms have inherent sequential steps that cannot be divided into independent sub-tasks. Parallelizing these algorithms requires careful consideration and often a complete redesign of the algorithm.

- Randomness and Reproducibility: Many machine learning algorithms rely on random processes. Parallelizing these algorithms can lead to challenges in ensuring that the results are reproducible. Different processors might generate different random numbers, leading to inconsistencies in the results.

- Integration with Dask: While Dask provides tools for parallelizing computations, integrating it with scikit-learn requires careful consideration of the above challenges. Dask-ML, a library that extends Dask to parallelize machine learning algorithms, provides solutions to some of these challenges but still requires understanding and careful handling of the underlying complexities.

While parallelizing scikit-learn models can lead to significant performance gains, it also introduces a host of challenges that must be carefully considered and addressed. Understanding these challenges may or may not be the first step towards effectively leveraging parallel computing in scikit-learn. However, we will begin straight to action in parallelizing the models in further sections.

Parallelizing Scikit-learn Models

Parallelizing scikit-learn models with Dask can be achieved through Dask-ML, a library that provides scalable machine learning in Python using Dask alongside existing machine learning libraries like scikit-learn.

Following is a step-wise walkthrough to parallelizing a scikit-learn model using Dask:

Import Libraries

First, import the necessary libraries, including Dask and Dask-ML.

```
from dask.distributed import Client
from dask_ml.model_selection import train_test_split
from sklearn.datasets import make_classification
from sklearn.ensemble import RandomForestClassifier
from dask_ml.wrappers import ParallelPostFit
```

Start Dask Client

Starting a Dask client will allow you to monitor and manage the parallel computations.

```
client = Client()
```

Create a Dataset

Create a synthetic dataset using scikit-learn's make_classification function. You can also load your dataset here.

```
X, y = make_classification(n_samples=10000, n_features=20, random_state=42)
```

Split the Data

Use Dask-ML's train_test_split to split the data into training and testing sets. This function works similarly to scikit-learn's version but operates lazily.

```
X_train, X_test, y_train, y_test = train_test_split(X, y, random_state=42)
```

Create a Scikit-Learn Model

Create a scikit-learn model as you normally would. In the below example, you can use a Random Forest Classifier.

```
model = RandomForestClassifier()
```

Wrap the Model with ParallelPostFit

Use Dask-ML's ParallelPostFit to wrap the scikit-learn model. This allows the model to be parallelized for predictions and transformations, while the fitting process remains the same.

```
parallel_model = ParallelPostFit(model)
```

Fit the Model

Fit the model to the training data. This step is performed using scikit-learn, not Dask, so it's not parallelized.

```
parallel_model.fit(X_train, y_train)
```

Make Predictions

Make predictions using the parallelized model. This step will be parallelized across the available cores or cluster.

```
predictions = parallel_model.predict(X_test)
```

Evaluate the Model

Evaluate the model using scikit-learn's metrics or any other desired method.

```
from sklearn.metrics import accuracy_score
accuracy = accuracy_score(y_test, predictions)
print("Accuracy:", accuracy)
```

This example demonstrates how to parallelize the prediction phase of a scikit-learn model using Dask and Dask-ML. The fitting process remains the same, but predictions and transformations are parallelized, allowing for scalable computations on large datasets.

Performing Model Selection

Model selection is an essential part of building machine learning models, and it involves choosing the best model and hyperparameters for a given problem. When working with large datasets, this process can be computationally expensive. Dask, in conjunction with scikit-learn, can parallelize this process, making it more efficient. Following is a step-wise walkthrough to performing model selection with Dask and scikit-learn:

Import Libraries
Import the necessary libraries, including Dask, Dask-ML, and scikit-learn.

```
from dask.distributed import Client
from dask_ml.model_selection import GridSearchCV
from sklearn.datasets import make_classification
from sklearn.ensemble import RandomForestClassifier
```

Start a Dask Client
Starting a Dask client will enable parallel computations.

```
client = Client()
```

Create a Dataset
Create or load your dataset. Here, you can create a synthetic dataset using scikit-learn's make_classification.

```
X, y = make_classification(n_samples=10000, n_features=20, random_state=42)
```

Define the Model

Define the scikit-learn model you want to use. In the below example, you can use a Random Forest Classifier.

```
model = RandomForestClassifier()
```

Define the Hyperparameter Grid

Define the grid of hyperparameters you want to search over. This could include various hyperparameters specific to the model you are using.

```
param_grid = {
   'n_estimators': [10, 50, 100],
   'max_depth': [None, 10, 20, 30],
   'min_samples_split': [2, 5, 10]
}
```

Create a GridSearchCV Object

Create a GridSearchCV object from Dask-ML, passing the model, parameter grid, and any other desired parameters like cross-validation strategy.

```
grid_search = GridSearchCV(model, param_grid, cv=5)
```

Fit the GridSearchCV Object

Fit the GridSearchCV object to the data. This step will perform cross-validation for each combination of hyperparameters in the grid, parallelizing the computations with Dask.

```
grid_search.fit(X, y)
```

Retrieve the Best Model

After fitting, you can retrieve the best model and its hyperparameters.

```
best_model = grid_search.best_estimator_
best_params = grid_search.best_params_
```

Use the Best Model

You can now use the best model for predictions, further evaluation, or any other purpose.

```
predictions = best_model.predict(X_test)
```

By using Dask-ML's GridSearchCV, you can perform hyperparameter tuning and model selection on large datasets in parallel, leveraging the power of Dask. This approach integrates seamlessly with scikit-learn, allowing you to scale your existing scikit-learn code to handle larger datasets without significant changes.

Running Model Evaluation

Model evaluation is a crucial step in the machine learning pipeline, allowing you to assess how well your model is performing. After parallelizing scikit-learn models with Dask and performing model selection, you can also evaluate the selected model using various metrics and techniques. Given below is how you can do it:

Split the Data

First, you'll need to split your data into training and testing sets to evaluate the model's performance on unseen data.

```
from sklearn.model_selection import train_test_split

X_train, X_test, y_train, y_test = train_test_split(X, y, test_size=0.2, random_state=42)
```

Fit the Best Model

Using the best model obtained from the previous step, fit it to the training data.

```
best_model.fit(X_train, y_train)
```

Make Predictions

Use the fitted model to make predictions on the test set.

```
y_pred = best_model.predict(X_test)
```

Compute Accuracy

You can compute the accuracy of the model using scikit-learn's accuracy_score function.

```
from sklearn.metrics import accuracy_score

accuracy = accuracy_score(y_test, y_pred)
print(f"Accuracy: {accuracy}")
```

Compute Other Metrics

Depending on the problem and the model, you may want to compute other metrics such as precision, recall, F1-score, ROC AUC, etc.

```
from sklearn.metrics import precision_score, recall_score, f1_score

precision = precision_score(y_test, y_pred)
recall = recall_score(y_test, y_pred)
f1 = f1_score(y_test, y_pred)

print(f"Precision: {precision}")
print(f"Recall: {recall}")
print(f"F1 Score: {f1}")
```

Confusion Matrix

A confusion matrix can provide a detailed breakdown of the model's performance across different classes.

```
from sklearn.metrics import confusion_matrix
import seaborn as sns
import matplotlib.pyplot as plt

conf_matrix = confusion_matrix(y_test, y_pred)
sns.heatmap(conf_matrix, annot=True)
plt.show()
```

Cross-Validation (Optional)

You can also perform cross-validation to get a more robust estimate of the model's performance.

```
from dask_ml.model_selection import cross_val_score

cv_scores = cross_val_score(best_model, X, y, cv=5)
print(f"Cross-Validation Scores: {cv_scores}")
```

Model evaluation is essential to understand how well your model is performing and where it might be lacking. By using scikit-learn's extensive metrics library in conjunction with Dask, you can efficiently evaluate your model on large datasets. These metrics and visualizations provide valuable insights into the model's behavior and can walkthrough further tuning and refinement.

Hyperparameter Tuning

Hyperparameter tuning is a critical step in building a robust machine learning model. It involves finding the optimal set of hyperparameters that produce the best performance for a given model. When working with large datasets and complex models, hyperparameter tuning can be computationally expensive. Dask can help parallelize this process, making it more efficient. Given below is how you can perform hyperparameter tuning using Dask and scikit-learn:

Define the Hyperparameter Grid

First, you'll need to define the range of hyperparameters you want to search. This can be done using a dictionary where the keys are the hyperparameter names, and the values are lists or distributions of the values to search.

```
param_grid = {
    'n_estimators': [50, 100, 200],
    'max_depth': [None, 10, 20, 30],
    'min_samples_split': [2, 5, 10],
    'min_samples_leaf': [1, 2, 4]
}
```

Create a Dask Client

You'll need a Dask client to distribute the computation across your cluster.

```python
from dask.distributed import Client

client = Client()
```

Create a Scikit-Learn Estimator
Create the scikit-learn estimator you want to tune. This could be a classifier, regressor, or any other model that has hyperparameters.

```python
from sklearn.ensemble import RandomForestClassifier

model = RandomForestClassifier()
```

Use Dask's GridSearchCV or RandomizedSearchCV
Dask provides parallelized versions of scikit-learn's GridSearchCV and RandomizedSearchCV that can be used in the same way.

```python
from dask_ml.model_selection import GridSearchCV

grid_search = GridSearchCV(model, param_grid, cv=5)
```

Fit the Model
Fit the grid search object to your data. This will perform the hyperparameter search in parallel using Dask.

```python
grid_search.fit(X_train, y_train)
```

Retrieve the Best Parameters
Once the search is complete, you can retrieve the best set of hyperparameters and the best model.

```python
best_params = grid_search.best_params_
best_model = grid_search.best_estimator_

print(f"Best Parameters: {best_params}")
```

Evaluate the Best Model

You can now evaluate the best model on your test set using the techniques taught in the previous section. Hyperparameter tuning is an essential step in building a robust and high-performing machine learning model. The process is very similar to using scikit-learn's tools, making it easy to integrate into your existing workflow.

Preprocessing and Feature Extraction

Preprocessing and feature extraction are essential steps in the machine learning pipeline. They transform raw data into a format that can be fed into machine learning algorithms. When dealing with large datasets, these steps can be computationally intensive. Dask can help parallelize these operations, making them more efficient. Given below is how you can perform preprocessing and feature extraction using Dask and scikit-learn:

Load Your Data

You can load your data into a Dask DataFrame. This allows you to work with larger-than-memory datasets.

```
import dask.dataframe as dd

data = dd.read_csv('data.csv')
```

Preprocessing

Preprocessing may include handling missing values, scaling features, encoding categorical variables, etc. Dask provides methods that parallelize these operations.

Handling Missing Values

You can use Dask's fillna method to fill missing values.

```
data = data.fillna(value=0)
```

Scaling Features

You can use scikit-learn's preprocessing functions along with Dask's map_partitions method to scale features.

```
from sklearn.preprocessing import StandardScaler
```

```
scaler = StandardScaler()
data_scaled = data.map_partitions(scaler.fit_transform)
```

Feature Extraction

Feature extraction involves transforming high-dimensional data into a lower-dimensional form. This can be done using techniques like Principal Component Analysis (PCA).

Using PCA with Dask

You can use Dask-ML's PCA implementation to perform this in parallel.

```
from dask_ml.decomposition import PCA

pca = PCA(n_components=5)
data_pca = pca.fit_transform(data_scaled)
```

Splitting the Data

You can use Dask's random_split method to split the data into training and test sets.

```
X_train, X_test, y_train, y_test = data_pca.random_split([0.8, 0.2])
```

Build and Train the Model

You can now build and train your scikit-learn model using the preprocessed and feature-extracted data, as taught in previous sections.

Preprocessing and feature extraction transforms raw data into a format suitable for machine learning algorithms. By leveraging Dask's parallel computing capabilities, you can efficiently handle these steps, especially when working with large datasets.

Understanding Large-scale Machine Learning

The case study provided at Dask official site demonstrates how Dask can be used with scikit-learn to perform large-scale machine learning. It's a comprehensive example that covers various aspects of parallelizing machine learning tasks. We shall now break down the case study and understand how it was implemented:

The case study focuses on training a machine learning model on a large dataset that doesn't fit into memory. The goal is to demonstrate how Dask can be used to parallelize computations and work with large datasets efficiently. The dataset used in the example is generated using the make_classification function from scikit-learn. It's a synthetic dataset with 100,000 samples and 20 features.

The case study is available in the following URL:
https://examples.dask.org/machine-learning/scale-scikit-learn.html

Dask Client

The example starts by setting up a Dask client, which provides a dashboard to monitor the computation.

```
from dask.distributed import Client

client = Client()
```

Data Preparation

The data is created using Dask's delayed function, which allows for lazy evaluation. This means that the computations are not executed immediately but are scheduled to run in parallel.

```
from dask_ml.datasets import make_classification

X, y = make_classification(n_samples=100000, n_features=20,
            chunks=1000, random_state=0)
```

Model Training

The example uses the Incremental meta-estimator from Dask-ML. This allows training a scikit-learn estimator on a large dataset incrementally.

```
from dask_ml.wrappers import Incremental
from sklearn.linear_model import SGDClassifier

estimator = SGDClassifier(random_state=0)
clf = Incremental(estimator)
clf.fit(X, y, classes=[0, 1])
```

Prediction and Evaluation

The trained model can be used to make predictions and evaluate its performance using standard scikit-learn metrics.

```
from sklearn.metrics import accuracy_score

y_pred = clf.predict(X)
accuracy = accuracy_score(y.compute(), y_pred.compute())
```

Hyperparameter Tuning

The example also demonstrates hyperparameter tuning using Dask's HyperbandSearchCV. It's an adaptive model selection method that can be used with scikit-learn estimators.

```
from dask_ml.model_selection import HyperbandSearchCV

params = {'alpha': [0.1, 0.01, 0.001]}
search = HyperbandSearchCV(estimator, params)
search.fit(X, y, classes=[0, 1])
```

The case study illustrates how Dask can be integrated with scikit-learn to perform large-scale machine learning. By using Dask's parallel computing capabilities, you can work with datasets that don't fit into memory and efficiently train models. The example covers various aspects, including data preparation, model training, prediction, evaluation, and hyperparameter tuning, providing a comprehensive walkthrough to scaling machine learning with Dask and scikit-learn.

Scikit-learn Best Practices

Integrating Dask with Scikit-Learn for parallel computing and handling large datasets is a powerful approach, but it requires careful consideration of best practices to confirm efficiency and effectiveness. The given below is a detailed highlights of the best practices for using Dask with Scikit-Learn:

Understanding the Data Size and Distribution

- Partitioning: Divide the data into suitable chunks or partitions that fit into memory. Dask's ability to handle data lazily allows for efficient processing of large datasets.

- Balancing: Ensure that the data is evenly distributed across partitions to avoid workload imbalance, which can lead to inefficient utilization of resources.

Utilizing Dask's Lazy Evaluation

- Delayed Computations: Use Dask's delayed function to build computation graphs without executing them immediately. This allows for optimization and parallel execution.

- Task Graph Optimization: Visualize and understand the task graph to identify bottlenecks and optimize the flow of computations.

Model Training and Incremental Learning

- Incremental Training: Use Dask-ML's Incremental wrapper for training Scikit-Learn models incrementally on large datasets.

- Batch Processing: Process data in batches that fit into memory, and use Dask's parallel capabilities to handle these batches efficiently.

Hyperparameter Tuning

- Dask-ML's SearchCV: Utilize Dask-ML's implementations of cross-validated hyperparameter search, like HyperbandSearchCV, to parallelize hyperparameter tuning across a cluster.

Monitoring and Resource Management

- Dask Dashboard: Utilize the Dask dashboard to monitor the cluster's performance, identify bottlenecks, and understand task execution.

- Resource Constraints: Set appropriate resource constraints to confirm that tasks are allocated efficiently across the cluster.

Error Handling and Debugging

- Logging: Implement proper logging to track errors and performance issues.

- Testing: Test the code with smaller datasets before scaling up to confirm that the logic is correct.

Integration with Other Libraries

- Compatibility: Ensure compatibility between Dask and Scikit-Learn versions.

- Utilizing Other Libraries: Consider integrating Dask with other libraries like Numba, Xarray, or Pandas when appropriate, as demonstrated in previous chapters.

Scalability Considerations

- Scaling Up and Down: Understand when to scale the cluster up or down based on the workload and data size.

- Distributed Computing: Utilize Dask's distributed scheduler when working across multiple machines to leverage parallel computing effectively.

Performance Profiling

- Benchmarking: Regularly benchmark the performance to identify areas for optimization.

- Profiling Tools: Utilize Dask's built-in profiling tools to analyze performance and identify bottlenecks.

By adhering to these best practices, one can confirm efficient utilization of resources, effective model training, and robust error handling. Continuous monitoring, understanding the underlying architecture, and thoughtful integration with other tools are key to maximizing the benefits of using Dask with Scikit-Learn.

Summary

In this chapter, we delved into the integration of Dask with Scikit-Learn, focusing on parallelizing machine learning tasks. We began by understanding the challenges of parallelizing Scikit-Learn models and how Dask can overcome these limitations. Practical examples were provided to demonstrate parallelizing Scikit-Learn models, model selection, evaluation, hyperparameter tuning, and preprocessing and feature extraction using Dask. The chapter also included a detailed case study showcasing large-scale machine learning implementation with Dask and Scikit-Learn.

The chapter further explored best practices for using Dask with Scikit-Learn, emphasizing the importance of understanding data size and distribution, utilizing Dask's lazy evaluation, model training, hyperparameter tuning, monitoring, resource management, error handling, integration with other libraries, scalability considerations, and performance profiling. These practices were elaborated to walkthrough the efficient and effective use of Dask in conjunction with Scikit-Learn for parallel computing. The insights provided a comprehensive view of how to maximize the benefits of using Dask with Scikit-Learn.

Overall, the chapter provided a thorough understanding of how Dask can be coupled with Scikit-Learn to perform parallel processing of machine learning operations. Through practical examples, detailed explanations, and a focus on best practices, the chapter offered valuable insights into leveraging Dask's capabilities with Scikit-Learn. The knowledge gained from this chapter equips the reader with the skills and understanding needed to apply Dask in real-world machine learning scenarios, optimizing performance, and handling large-scale data efficiently.

Chapter 8: Integrated Libraries: Dask and PyTorch

PyTorch Overview

PyTorch, an open-source deep learning framework developed by Facebook's AI Research lab, has rapidly gained popularity among researchers, data scientists, and deep learning professionals. This comprehensive overview delves into PyTorch's key features and its substantial contributions to the field of deep learning:

Dynamic Computation Graphs

Unlike many other deep learning frameworks that rely on static computation graphs, PyTorch employs dynamic computation graphs. This unique feature allows the computational graph to be constructed in real-time as operations are executed. This dynamic nature offers unparalleled flexibility and makes debugging significantly easier, thereby accelerating the development process.

Tensors: The Building Blocks

At the heart of PyTorch are tensors, its core data structure. These are akin to NumPy arrays but come with the added advantage of GPU compatibility. Tensors are crucial for efficient numerical computations and serve as the foundational elements for constructing neural networks.

GPU Acceleration

PyTorch offers seamless GPU integration, enabling computational tasks to be transferred to GPUs for remarkable speed enhancements. This GPU acceleration is particularly vital for training intricate deep learning models that require substantial computational resources.

Autograd: Automatic Differentiation

The Autograd library is another standout feature of PyTorch. It automatically calculates gradients for tensor operations, a critical component for gradient-based optimization algorithms like stochastic gradient descent (SGD), which are used extensively in neural network training.

Rich Ecosystem and Libraries

PyTorch boasts a diverse ecosystem that includes a plethora of libraries and tools designed for specialized tasks. For instance, TorchVision is tailored for computer vision applications, TorchText is designed for natural language processing, and TorchAudio focuses on audio data processing.

Research-Centric Design

PyTorch's dynamic and intuitive architecture makes it a preferred choice among the research community. It facilitates rapid prototyping and experimentation, thereby serving as a catalyst for innovative research in deep learning.

Seamless Transition to Production

With the advent of TorchScript, PyTorch has bridged the gap between research and production. TorchScript enables the serialization and optimization of models, allowing them to be deployed efficiently across diverse environments.

Robust Community and Support

One of PyTorch's greatest assets is its vibrant and ever-growing community. This includes a mix of developers, researchers, and practitioners who actively contribute to the framework. Comprehensive documentation, in-depth tutorials, and active forums offer invaluable support to users of all expertise levels.

Dask Integration for Distributed Training

PyTorch's capabilities are further extended through its integration with Dask, a parallel computing library. Dask facilitates distributed training across multiple GPUs and machines, enabling the training of large-scale models on massive datasets.

Interoperability with Other Frameworks

PyTorch confirms smooth interoperability with several other popular libraries and frameworks. This includes ONNX for model interchange, NumPy for numerical operations, and TensorFlow for utilizing specific functionalities.

Overall, PyTorch stands out for its dynamic computation graphs, GPU-accelerated operations, and a rich ecosystem that supports both research and production. Its user-friendly design, coupled with robust community backing, has led to its widespread adoption in academia and industry alike. The framework's compatibility with tools like Dask further amplifies its versatility, making it an ideal choice for the development and deployment of state-of-the-art deep learning models.

Using PyTorch with Dask

Integrating PyTorch with Dask allows you to leverage distributed computing capabilities, enabling parallel training across multiple GPUs or machines. Following is a step-wise walkthrough to integrating PyTorch with Dask using a simple example:

Import Libraries

First, import the necessary libraries, including PyTorch and Dask.

```
import torch
import torch.nn as nn
```

```
import torch.optim as optim
from torch.utils.data import DataLoader
from dask_pytorch_ddp import data
from dask.distributed import Client
```

Define the Model

Create a simple neural network model using PyTorch. The given below is a practical illustration of a feedforward neural network with one hidden layer:

```
class SimpleNN(nn.Module):
    def __init__(self, input_size, hidden_size, output_size):
        super(SimpleNN, self).__init__()
        self.hidden = nn.Linear(input_size, hidden_size)
        self.relu = nn.ReLU()
        self.output = nn.Linear(hidden_size, output_size)

    def forward(self, x):
        x = self.hidden(x)
        x = self.relu(x)
        x = self.output(x)
        return x
```

Create DataLoaders

You can create PyTorch DataLoaders for your training and validation datasets. Dask provides a data.Collator class to help with this:

```
collate_fn = data.Collator()
train_loader = DataLoader(train_dataset, batch_size=32, collate_fn=collate_fn)
valid_loader = DataLoader(valid_dataset, batch_size=32, collate_fn=collate_fn)
```

Connect to Dask Cluster

Create a Dask client to connect to your cluster:

```
client = Client("tcp://scheduler-address:8786")
```

Define Training Function

Create a training function that includes the model training logic:

```
def train(model, train_loader, criterion, optimizer):
    model.train()
    for batch_idx, (data, target) in enumerate(train_loader):
        optimizer.zero_grad()
        output = model(data)
        loss = criterion(output, target)
        loss.backward()
        optimizer.step()
```

Distributed Training with Dask

Use Dask to parallelize the training across the cluster:

```
from dask_pytorch_ddp import dispatch

model = SimpleNN(input_size=10, hidden_size=5, output_size=1)
criterion = nn.MSELoss()
optimizer = optim.SGD(model.parameters(), lr=0.01)

# Run the training function across the cluster
dispatch.run(client, train, model, train_loader, criterion, optimizer)
```

This code will distribute the training of the PyTorch model across the available workers in the Dask cluster.

Evaluate the Model

You can similarly define an evaluation function and use Dask to parallelize the evaluation across the cluster. Integrating PyTorch with Dask enables distributed training, allowing you to scale your deep learning models across multiple GPUs or machines. By following these steps, you can leverage the parallel computing capabilities of Dask to train more complex models on larger datasets efficiently.

Parallelizing Deep Learning Operations

We shall now dive deeper into how Dask parallelizes deep learning training with PyTorch. You can explore the key components that enable this parallelization and how they work together.

Dask Distributed Client

Dask's distributed client is the entry point for parallel execution. It connects to a Dask scheduler, which manages the distribution of tasks across worker nodes.

```
from dask.distributed import Client
client = Client("tcp://scheduler-address:8786")
```

Dask PyTorch DDP

Dask provides a package called dask_pytorch_ddp that integrates with PyTorch's Distributed Data Parallel (DDP) module. DDP parallelizes the training by splitting the dataset across multiple GPUs or machines and synchronizing the gradients.

Data Partitioning

Dask's data partitioning is key to parallelizing the training. It divides the dataset into smaller chunks, and each worker processes a chunk. Dask provides a data.Collator class to help with this:

```
from dask_pytorch_ddp import data
collate_fn = data.Collator()
train_loader = DataLoader(train_dataset, batch_size=32, collate_fn=collate_fn)
```

Model Training Function

The training function is defined as usual, but it will be executed on each worker node. The gradients are computed locally on each worker and then synchronized across all workers.

```
def train(model, train_loader, criterion, optimizer):
    model.train()
    for batch_idx, (data, target) in enumerate(train_loader):
        optimizer.zero_grad()
        output = model(data)
        loss = criterion(output, target)
        loss.backward()
```

```
optimizer.step()
```

Distributed Training with Dask

The dispatch.run function takes the training function and other parameters and distributes the training across the cluster:

```
from dask_pytorch_ddp import dispatch
dispatch.run(client, train, model, train_loader, criterion, optimizer)
```

Dask's parallelization of deep learning training with PyTorch is achieved through a combination of task scheduling, data partitioning, gradient synchronization, fault tolerance, and resource management.

Running PyTorch Model in Parallel

Running a PyTorch model in parallel with Dask involves several key steps, particularly in the areas of data loading and processing. Given below is a step-by-step walkthrough:

Import Necessary Libraries

Import the required libraries for PyTorch, Dask, and any data processing you'll need.

```
import torch
from torch.utils.data import DataLoader
from dask.distributed import Client
from dask_pytorch_ddp import data
```

Connect to Dask Cluster

Create a Dask client that connects to the cluster where you want to run the parallel computations.

```
client = Client("tcp://scheduler-address:8786")
```

Define Dataset and Transformations

Define the PyTorch dataset and any transformations you want to apply to the data. This could include normalization, augmentation, etc.

```python
from torchvision import datasets, transforms

transform = transforms.Compose([
    transforms.ToTensor(),
    transforms.Normalize((0.5,), (0.5,))
])

train_dataset = datasets.MNIST('.', download=True, transform=transform)
```

Create Dask Collator
Dask provides a data.Collator class that helps in partitioning the data across the workers.

```python
collate_fn = data.Collator()
```

Create Data Loader
Create a PyTorch DataLoader, specifying the dataset, batch size, and the Dask collator function.

```python
train_loader = DataLoader(train_dataset, batch_size=32, collate_fn=collate_fn)
```

Define the Model
Define the PyTorch model that you want to train. This could be any neural network architecture suitable for your task.

```python
model = torch.nn.Sequential(
    torch.nn.Linear(784, 128),
    torch.nn.ReLU(),
    torch.nn.Linear(128, 10),
)
```

Define Training Function
Create the training function that will be run on each worker. This includes the forward pass, loss computation, and backward pass.

```python
def train(model, train_loader, criterion, optimizer):
```

```
model.train()
for batch_idx, (data, target) in enumerate(train_loader):
    optimizer.zero_grad()
    output = model(data)
    loss = criterion(output, target)
    loss.backward()
    optimizer.step()
```

Distributed Training with Dask

Use Dask's dispatch.run function to distribute the training across the cluster.

```
from dask_pytorch_ddp import dispatch

criterion = torch.nn.CrossEntropyLoss()
optimizer = torch.optim.SGD(model.parameters(), lr=0.01)

dispatch.run(client, train, model, train_loader, criterion, optimizer)
```

These steps outline how to perform data loading and processing when running a PyTorch model in parallel with Dask.

Distributed Training of PyTorch Model

Continuing from the previous steps, we shall delve into the practical aspects of performing distributed training of a PyTorch model using Dask.

Define Distributed Data Sampler

When working with distributed training, you'll need to confirm that the data is evenly distributed across the workers. You can use torch.utils.data.distributed.DistributedSampler for this purpose.

```
from torch.utils.data.distributed import DistributedSampler

sampler = DistributedSampler(train_dataset)
train_loader = DataLoader(train_dataset, batch_size=32, sampler=sampler, collate_fn=collate_fn)
```

Initialize Distributed Environment

You'll need to initialize the distributed environment using torch.distributed.init_process_group. This sets up the communication between the different workers.

```
import torch.distributed as dist

dist.init_process_group(backend='nccl')
```

Create Distributed Data Parallel Model

Wrap your model with torch.nn.parallel.DistributedDataParallel to enable parallel training across multiple GPUs.

```
device = torch.device("cuda" if torch.cuda.is_available() else "cpu")
model.to(device)
model = torch.nn.parallel.DistributedDataParallel(model)
```

Modify Training Function for Distributed Training

Update the training function to handle distributed training. This includes moving the data to the correct device.

```
def train(model, train_loader, criterion, optimizer):
    model.train()
    for batch_idx, (data, target) in enumerate(train_loader):
        data, target = data.to(device), target.to(device)
        optimizer.zero_grad()
        output = model(data)
        loss = criterion(output, target)
        loss.backward()
        optimizer.step()
```

Run Distributed Training with Dask

You can now run the distributed training using Dask's dispatch.run function as before.

```
dispatch.run(client, train, model, train_loader, criterion, optimizer)
```

Gather Results

After training, you may want to gather the results from all workers. You can use Dask's client.gather method for this.

```
results = client.gather(results)
```

By following these steps, you can leverage the power of parallel computing to train deep learning models more efficiently and on larger datasets. This approach is particularly valuable for training complex models that would be too time-consuming or resource-intensive to train on a single machine.

Model Evaluation and Hyperparameter Tuning

Continuing from the distributed training of a PyTorch model with Dask, we shall explore how to perform model evaluation and hyperparameter tuning.

Model Evaluation

Define Evaluation Function

You'll need to define a function to evaluate the model on a validation or test dataset. This function should handle distributed evaluation as well.

```
def evaluate(model, val_loader, criterion):
    model.eval()
    val_loss = 0
    correct = 0
    with torch.no_grad():
        for data, target in val_loader:
            data, target = data.to(device), target.to(device)
            output = model(data)
            val_loss += criterion(output, target).item()
            pred = output.argmax(dim=1, keepdim=True)
            correct += pred.eq(target.view_as(pred)).sum().item()

    val_loss /= len(val_loader.dataset)
```

```
    accuracy = correct / len(val_loader.dataset)
    return val_loss, accuracy
```

Run Evaluation with Dask

You can run the evaluation function using Dask's dispatch.run method.

```
val_loss, accuracy = dispatch.run(client, evaluate, model, val_loader, criterion)
```

Hyperparameter Tuning

Define Hyperparameter Search Space

You can define the hyperparameter search space using libraries like Scikit-Learn or Optuna. The given below is a practical illustration using Scikit-Learn's GridSearchCV.

```
from sklearn.model_selection import GridSearchCV

param_grid = {
    'learning_rate': [0.01, 0.001],
    'batch_size': [32, 64],
}
```

Wrap PyTorch Model for Scikit-Learn

You'll need to wrap your PyTorch model to make it compatible with Scikit-Learn's API. You can use skorch library for this.

```
from skorch import NeuralNetClassifier

net = NeuralNetClassifier(model, max_epochs=10, lr=0.01)
```

Run Grid Search with Dask

You can run the grid search using Dask's GridSearchCV.

```
from dask_ml.model_selection import GridSearchCV

grid_search = GridSearchCV(net, param_grid, scoring='accuracy', cv=5)
```

```
grid_search.fit(X_train, y_train)
```

Retrieve Best Parameters

You can retrieve the best hyperparameters from the grid search.

```
best_params = grid_search.best_params_
```

Model evaluation and hyperparameter tuning in a distributed environment with Dask and PyTorch involve additional considerations to confirm that the computations are properly parallelized. By following these steps, you can efficiently evaluate your model and tune hyperparameters across multiple GPUs or machines, leveraging the full power of your hardware to find the optimal model configuration.

PyTorch Best Practices

Integrating Dask with PyTorch for parallel and distributed deep learning involves several considerations. The given below is a detailed highlights of the best practices for using Dask with PyTorch:

Understanding the Distributed Environment

- Cluster Configuration: Choose the right cluster configuration based on the workload. Dask supports different cluster managers like Kubernetes, YARN, or SLURM, which can be tailored to your needs.

- Data Distribution: Ensure that the data is evenly distributed across the cluster to prevent any worker from becoming a bottleneck.

Data Loading and Preprocessing

- Dask Arrays and DataFrames: Utilize Dask's data structures for efficient parallel data loading and preprocessing.

- Chunking: Break the data into manageable chunks that fit into the memory of individual workers.

- Data Locality: Store data close to the computation to minimize data transfer times.

Model Parallelism

- Model Distribution: Distribute the model across multiple GPUs or nodes to parallelize the training.

- Synchronization: Use Dask's synchronization primitives to confirm that the model parameters are updated consistently across all replicas.

Training and Evaluation

- Batch Sizing: Adjust the batch size according to the number of workers to maintain the GPU utilization.

- Monitoring: Utilize Dask's dashboard to monitor the training process, resource utilization, and identify potential bottlenecks.

- Evaluation: Parallelize the evaluation process using Dask to reduce the validation time.

Hyperparameter Tuning

- Parallel Search: Use Dask's integration with hyperparameter search libraries like GridSearchCV to parallelize the search process.

- Search Space: Define a reasonable search space to confirm that the search is both comprehensive and efficient.

Fault Tolerance and Scalability

- Recovery: Implement mechanisms to recover from worker failures, such as saving checkpoints.

- Scaling: Utilize Dask's dynamic scaling to add or remove workers based on the workload.

Integration with Other Libraries

- Compatibility: Ensure compatibility with other libraries like scikit-learn or Numba by using appropriate wrappers or connectors.

Performance Optimization

- Task Fusion: Utilize Dask's task fusion to combine multiple tasks into a single task, reducing overhead.
- Communication: Minimize inter-worker communication by organizing computations to reduce data transfers.

Testing and Debugging

- Local Testing: Test the code locally using Dask's local cluster before deploying to a distributed environment.

- Logging: Implement proper logging to facilitate debugging in a distributed setting.

By following these best practices, developers can confirm that they are leveraging the full potential of both libraries while maintaining code quality, efficiency, and scalability. These practices walkthrough the integration of Dask and PyTorch, from data loading to model training, evaluation, hyperparameter tuning, and beyond, providing a comprehensive framework for parallel and distributed deep learning.

Summary

In this chapter, we explored the synergy between Dask and PyTorch, with a special focus on parallelizing the training of deep learning models. We started by examining the core features of the PyTorch framework and its pivotal role in the realm of deep learning. The spotlight was then turned to how Dask complements PyTorch by enabling parallel and scalable training workflows.

Transitioning to hands-on applications, we learned various operational facets such as data ingestion, preprocessing, distributed model training, performance evaluation, and hyperparameter optimization. Each of these elements was elaborated upon, underscoring the ways in which Dask amplifies their efficiency. Additionally, the section featured an in-depth walkthrough on best practices for harmonizing Dask and PyTorch. These encompassed topics like configuring your computing cluster, distributing data effectively, implementing model parallelism, optimizing batch sizes, ensuring fault tolerance, and fine-tuning performance.

Towards the end, we delved into specialized techniques like work stealing, task fusion, and dynamic task scheduling, which further optimize the parallel training process. We also touched upon how Dask seamlessly integrates with other libraries and platforms, highlighting its versatility and collaborative potential. All in all, this section served as a comprehensive primer on leveraging Dask's capabilities to enhance PyTorch-based deep learning projects, complete with practical examples and actionable best practices.

Chapter 9: Dask with GPUs

Understanding GPU Computing

Central Processing Units (CPUs) have long served as the cornerstone of general-purpose computing, engineered to manage a broad spectrum of tasks. These units excel in executing instructions sequentially and are typically outfitted with a limited number of cores that are highly optimized for logical control, arithmetic calculations, and task switching. This makes them particularly well-suited for computational-heavy tasks that demand multitasking capabilities but don't necessarily benefit from parallel processing. Over the years, CPUs have evolved to become more efficient and powerful, but their architecture remains fundamentally geared towards sequential processing.

In contrast, Graphics Processing Units (GPUs) usher in a radically different computing paradigm centered around parallelism. Originally conceived to manage the demands of graphics rendering—a task that inherently calls for the simultaneous processing of countless pixels—GPUs have evolved to feature hundreds or even thousands of smaller, more efficient cores specifically engineered for parallel execution. These cores are fine-tuned to handle data-parallel tasks, executing identical operations across multiple data points concurrently. This architectural difference between CPUs and GPUs is not just a matter of core count; it's a fundamental divergence in design philosophy and operational efficiency.

This shift towards GPU-based computing has had a transformative impact on various specialized fields, most notably deep learning, scientific simulations, and large-scale data analysis. In these areas, the capacity for parallel processing is invaluable. For instance, training intricate deep learning models can be an exceedingly time-consuming endeavor when relying solely on a CPU. However, the parallel computing capabilities of a GPU can dramatically accelerate this process, reducing training times from days to hours or even minutes. This speed-up is not just a matter of convenience; it often enables more complex and accurate models, thereby advancing the field as a whole.

Moreover, the utility of GPU computing extends far beyond these specialized applications. In today's computing landscape, GPUs are increasingly being deployed alongside CPUs in a hybrid computational model to boost a wide array of applications. This spans everything from video game rendering and virtual reality simulations to business intelligence analytics and real-time financial modeling. In this hybrid model, the CPU continues to manage general-purpose tasks that require complex logic and multitasking, while the GPU is unleashed on tasks that can be parallelized. This collaborative approach capitalizes on the unique strengths of both types of processors, offering a balanced and highly efficient computing environment.

To sum up, while CPUs continue to play a crucial role in general-purpose computing and complex logical operations, GPUs have carved out an indispensable niche in tasks requiring high-throughput parallel processing. The symbiotic relationship between CPUs and GPUs in modern computing architectures represents a holistic approach that optimizes performance across a diverse range of tasks. This dual-processor ecosystem is shaping the future of computing, driving innovations and efficiencies that are transforming industries and paving the way for new technological breakthroughs.

Dask for GPU Computing

Dask's integration with GPU computing represents a significant advancement in parallel and distributed computing. For a comprehensive understanding of how Dask synergizes with GPU computing, we shall delve into various facets that make this integration so powerful:

GPU Compatibility

Dask offers native support for GPU computing through its integration with specialized libraries such as CuPy, RAPIDS, and Numba. These libraries act as the bridge that allows Dask to offload specific computational tasks to the GPU, thereby taking full advantage of the GPU's parallel processing capabilities. This seamless integration makes it easier for developers to write GPU-accelerated code without having to deal with the intricacies of GPU programming.

Distributed GPU Computing Architecture

One of Dask's standout features is its distributed scheduler, which is capable of orchestrating GPU resources across multiple nodes in a cluster. This enables Dask to perform large-scale parallel computations that can span multiple GPUs across different machines, thereby significantly boosting computational throughput.

Dask GPU Arrays

Dask has the ability to create and manage GPU arrays through libraries like CuPy. These arrays are conceptually similar to NumPy arrays but are designed to reside in the GPU's memory space. Dask can execute parallel operations on these arrays, effectively harnessing the computational power of the GPU's multiple cores.

GPU-Accelerated DataFrames

Dask integrates seamlessly with RAPIDS cuDF to support GPU DataFrames. These specialized DataFrames are designed for parallel processing of large tabular datasets directly on the GPU. This enables faster data manipulation and analysis, which is particularly beneficial for data-intensive applications.

Task Graph Representation

In Dask, computations are represented as a directed acyclic graph (DAG) of tasks. When operating in a GPU environment, these tasks are enriched to include GPU-specific operations, such as data transfers between CPU and GPU memory or between GPUs on different nodes.

Intelligent GPU Scheduling

Dask's scheduler is not just capable but also GPU-aware. It intelligently assigns tasks to available GPUs based on various factors, including memory requirements, data locality, and computational complexity. This confirms optimal utilization of GPU resources.

Asynchronous Execution for Efficiency

Dask supports asynchronous execution, a feature that allows for the overlapping of computation and communication tasks. This is particularly important for maximizing GPU utilization, as it prevents the GPU from sitting idle while waiting for data transfers or other tasks to complete.

GPU Memory Management

Dask can manage a dedicated pool of GPU memory, dynamically allocating and deallocating memory resources as tasks require. This memory pooling mechanism helps in reducing memory fragmentation and minimizes the overhead associated with frequent memory allocation and deallocation.

Efficient Data Transfers

Data transfer is a critical aspect of any distributed computing environment, and Dask excels in this area. It efficiently manages data transfers between the CPU and GPU memory and also handles inter-GPU communication across different machines. This is vital for maintaining high performance in distributed GPU setups.

Dask and Deep Learning Frameworks

Dask's capabilities extend to the realm of deep learning as well. It can parallelize the training process in deep learning frameworks like PyTorch and TensorFlow. By distributing the training workload across multiple GPUs, Dask accelerates the training process, making it more efficient and scalable.

Performing GPU Computing with Dask

We shall now explore GPU-Accelerated Computing using Dask by adapting one of the previous examples. You can use a simple matrix multiplication operation, which can be parallelized using Dask and executed on the GPU.

Importing Libraries

CuPy: A GPU-accelerated library for numerical computations that is compatible with NumPy.
Dask: For parallelizing the computations.

```
import cupy as cp
import dask.array as da
```

Creating GPU Arrays with CuPy

You can create two large matrices using CuPy, which will reside in GPU memory.

```
A_gpu = cp.random.rand(10000, 10000)
B_gpu = cp.random.rand(10000, 10000)
```

Creating Dask Arrays from GPU Arrays

You can wrap the CuPy arrays with Dask to create Dask arrays. This allows us to use Dask's parallel computing capabilities with GPU data.

```
A_dask = da.from_array(A_gpu, chunks=(2000, 2000))
B_dask = da.from_array(B_gpu, chunks=(2000, 2000))
```

Matrix Multiplication

You can perform matrix multiplication using Dask's dot function. This operation will be parallelized across the available GPU cores.

```
C_dask = da.dot(A_dask, B_dask)
```

Computation

You can call the compute method to execute the computation. This will build a task graph and execute it on the GPU.

```
C_gpu = C_dask.compute()
```

This sample illustrates the utilization of GPU-accelerated computing through the integration of Dask and CuPy. By combining these technologies, we can tap into the GPUs' parallel processing capabilities for efficient execution of extensive calculations. The fusion of Dask's capacity for parallel computing with GPU speed-up creates a robust instrument for tasks in scientific computing, machine learning, and other data-heavy applications.

What is RAPIDS?

RAPIDS is an open-source suite of data processing and machine learning libraries that enable GPU acceleration for data science workflows. It is designed to provide a GPU-native, high-performance, and easy-to-use platform for data scientists and developers. RAPIDS builds on popular Python libraries like Pandas, Scikit-Learn, and Dask, offering GPU-accelerated versions that are fully compatible with their API.

Core Components

The core components of RAPIDS include:

- cuDF: A GPU-accelerated data manipulation library that mimics the Pandas DataFrame API.

- cuML: A GPU-accelerated machine learning library that provides GPU versions of Scikit-Learn algorithms.

- cuGraph: A GPU-accelerated graph analytics library.

- cuSpatial: A GPU-accelerated spatial and spatiotemporal data processing library.

Dask's Integration with RAPIDS

Dask's integration with RAPIDS enables distributed, parallel, and GPU-accelerated data processing and machine learning workflows. The given below is how you can leverage this integration:

Importing Libraries

Import the necessary RAPIDS and Dask libraries.

```
import dask_cudf
import dask_ml.model_selection as dcv
from cuml.dask.ensemble import RandomForestClassifier
from dask.distributed import Client
from dask_cuda import LocalCUDACluster
```

Setting Up a Dask GPU Cluster

Create a Dask cluster that utilizes available GPUs.

```
cluster = LocalCUDACluster()
client = Client(cluster)
```

Loading Data with Dask cuDF
Load a dataset into a Dask cuDF DataFrame, which is distributed across GPUs.

```
ddf = dask_cudf.read_csv('data.csv')
```

Preprocessing
Perform preprocessing tasks using Dask cuDF, similar to how you would with Pandas.

```
X = ddf.drop('target', axis=1)
y = ddf['target']
```

Model Training
Train a distributed, GPU-accelerated machine learning model using cuML and Dask.

```
model = RandomForestClassifier()
model.fit(X, y)
```

Model Evaluation and Hyperparameter Tuning
Use Dask-ML for distributed hyperparameter tuning and model evaluation.

```
params = {'n_estimators': [10, 50, 100], 'max_depth': [5, 10, 15]}
grid_search = dcv.GridSearchCV(model, params)
grid_search.fit(X, y)
```

The fusion of Dask and RAPIDS creates a robust environment for executing data science tasks that are parallel, distributed, and optimized for GPU acceleration. Utilizing well-known APIs from Pandas and Scikit-Learn, in conjunction with Dask's ability to manage distributed computing, enables data scientists to effortlessly develop and scale applications that take advantage of GPU acceleration.

What is Google JAX?

Google JAX is an open-source numerical computing library that extends the capabilities of NumPy by enabling automatic differentiation and GPU/TPU acceleration. It's designed for high-performance machine learning research and has become popular for its flexibility and efficiency in scientific computing.

Core Features

JAX's core features include:

- Automatic Differentiation: JAX can automatically compute derivatives, gradients, and higher-order derivatives of functions, making it suitable for optimization and machine learning tasks.

- GPU/TPU Acceleration: JAX can run computations on GPUs and TPUs, offering significant speed-ups for numerical operations.

- Functional Programming: JAX encourages a functional programming paradigm, where functions are pure and stateless, leading to more maintainable and testable code.

- XLA Compilation: JAX uses XLA (Accelerated Linear Algebra), a domain-specific compiler for linear algebra, to optimize and parallelize computations across hardware devices.

Dask's Integration with Google JAX

Dask's integration with Google JAX allows for distributed and parallel execution of JAX computations across multiple GPUs or CPUs. This combination enables scalable and efficient numerical computing for large-scale problems. Following is a step-wise walkthrough to integrating Dask with JAX:

Importing Libraries

Import Dask and JAX libraries.

```
import jax
import jax.numpy as jnp
from dask.distributed import Client
```

Setting Up a Dask Cluster

Create a Dask cluster to distribute computations.

```
client = Client()
```

Defining a JAX Function

Define a function using JAX's NumPy extension, jax.numpy.

```
def my_function(x):
    return jnp.sin(x) * jnp.cos(x)
```

JIT Compilation

Use JAX's Just-In-Time (JIT) compilation to optimize the function for GPU execution.

```
jit_function = jax.jit(my_function)
```

Distributing Computations with Dask

Use Dask to distribute the JAX computations across the cluster.

```
from dask import delayed

# Create a Dask delayed object
delayed_result = delayed(jit_function)(jnp.array([1.0, 2.0, 3.0]))

# Compute the result
result = delayed_result.compute()
```

Leveraging JAX's capabilities for GPU acceleration, auto-differentiation, and functional programming, along with Dask's expertise in distributed computing, this integrated platform empowers researchers and data scientists to efficiently solve intricate numerical challenges.

Summary

In this chapter, we ventured into the intriguing domain of GPU computing, initiating our learnings with a side-by-side analysis of conventional CPU computing and its more contemporary counterpart, GPU computing. The latter brings to the table remarkable benefits in terms of parallel computation and processing speed, making it indispensable for tackling intricate numerical challenges. We delved into the structural intricacies of GPU computing to comprehend how it facilitates the concurrent execution of tasks, thereby optimizing the handling of extensive computational problems.

A focal point of our learnings was the synergy between Dask and GPU computing. We discovered how Dask is proficient in allocating computational tasks across multiple GPUs, thereby providing scalable solutions to large-scale numerical challenges. We scrutinized real-world instances of GPU-accelerated computing facilitated by Dask, particularly its collaboration with RAPIDS—an ensemble of software libraries designed to perform comprehensive data science and analytics workflows directly on GPUs. This amalgamation paves the way for expedited data manipulation and the training of machine learning algorithms.

In the concluding part of this section, we turned our attention to the collaboration between Dask and Google JAX, a computational library that augments NumPy with features like automatic differentiation and GPU/TPU support. Through hands-on examples, we guided the reader on how to configure a Dask cluster, formulate JAX functions, and distribute tasks via Dask. This confluence of technologies creates a robust framework for distributed and parallel numerical computing, marrying the GPU acceleration and automatic differentiation capabilities of JAX with Dask's expertise in distributed computing.

Chapter 10: Scaling Machine Learning Projects with Dask

Structure of Machine Learning Projects

Machine learning (ML) is a field of artificial intelligence that focuses on building systems that can learn from and make predictions or decisions based on data. It's a process that involves several key steps, each of which can be computationally intensive, especially when dealing with large datasets.

In this section, we offer a comprehensive exploration of the standard machine learning pipeline, emphasizing the computational aspects that underpin each stage. This will set the stage for our subsequent learnings on how Dask and its extended library, DaskML, can significantly optimize these processes, especially when dealing with large-scale data.

Data Collection

The initial phase involves amassing raw data from a multitude of sources, which could range from text and images to audio and video files. Given the sheer volume and intricacy of the data, substantial computing power is often necessary to manage and store it effectively. In some cases, real-time data collection may also be involved, adding another layer of computational complexity.

Data Preprocessing

Once the data is collected, the next step is to refine it. This involves a series of operations such as imputing missing values, normalizing numerical variables, encoding categorical variables, and even text preprocessing like tokenization in natural language processing tasks. The computational load at this stage can be quite high, particularly when the dataset is extensive or the transformations are complex.

Feature Engineering

This stage is about crafting new features from the existing dataset to enhance the predictive power of the machine learning model. Techniques could range from simple mathematical transformations to more complex operations like Fourier transforms or principal component analysis. The computational requirements here can be quite demanding, especially for high-dimensional data.

Model Training

Here, an algorithm is chosen based on the problem at hand, and the model is trained using the preprocessed and engineered data. This phase is often the most resource-intensive, particularly when dealing with deep learning architectures or massive datasets. The model undergoes multiple iterations to fine-tune its parameters, aiming to minimize a predefined loss function.

Model Evaluation

Post-training, the model's efficacy is gauged using a variety of metrics such as accuracy, F1-score, precision, recall, and many others. This involves running the model on a separate validation dataset and contrasting the predicted outcomes with the actual labels. Depending on the complexity of the model and the size of the validation set, this step can also be computationally intensive.

Hyperparameter Tuning

This involves the optimization of model settings, known as hyperparameters, to enhance performance. Techniques like grid search, random search, or even more advanced methods like Bayesian optimization are employed. Each run can be computationally expensive, as it involves training the model multiple times with varying configurations.

Deployment

After rigorous training and tuning, the model is finally deployed into a live environment. Here, it is expected to make real-time predictions, often requiring a robust computational infrastructure to handle a high volume of queries efficiently.

Monitoring and Maintenance

Post-deployment, the model needs to be continuously monitored to confirm it is performing as expected. This could involve periodic retraining, feature updates, or even complete model overhauls. Each of these activities has its own set of computational requirements.

In situations and challenges involving large datasets or complex models, each of these stages can pose significant computational challenges. This is where parallel and distributed computing techniques become indispensable. Tools like Dask offer scalable and efficient solutions for parallelizing many of these computationally intensive tasks.

As we transition to the next segment of this chapter, we will focus on DaskML, a specialized library that extends Dask's capabilities to facilitate scalable machine learning in Python. DaskML capitalizes on Dask's inherent strengths in parallel computing to manage the heavy computational lifting involved in machine learning, making it an ideal choice for large-scale data projects. Understanding the computational intricacies of the machine learning pipeline allows us to fully grasp the transformative impact that DaskML can have on the field.

Introduction to DaskML

DaskML is a powerful library designed to bridge the gap between parallel computing and machine learning. It leverages the capabilities of Dask, a parallel computing library in Python, to enable scalable machine learning. DaskML extends the parallel computing capabilities of Dask to the domain of machine learning. It provides scalable solutions for training and deploying machine learning models, particularly when dealing with large datasets that are beyond the capacity of a single machine.

Purpose of DaskML

- Scalable Machine Learning: DaskML enables the training of machine learning models on large datasets by distributing the computations across multiple cores or even multiple machines.

- Integration with Popular Libraries: It offers seamless integration with popular machine learning libraries like Scikit-Learn, enabling users to scale their existing code with minimal changes.

- Efficient Resource Utilization: By leveraging Dask's scheduling capabilities, DaskML assures efficient utilization of available resources, balancing the load across the cluster.

- Hyperparameter Tuning: DaskML provides tools for parallelized hyperparameter tuning, significantly reducing the time required to find the optimal model parameters.

How DaskML Functions

- Distributed Training: DaskML divides the dataset into smaller partitions and distributes them across the available computing resources. The model is then trained on these partitions in parallel, aggregating the results.

- Parallelized Preprocessing: It offers parallelized implementations of common preprocessing tasks, such as scaling and encoding, allowing for faster data preparation.

- Integration with Scikit-Learn: DaskML provides a set of estimators that are compatible with Scikit-Learn's API. This means that existing Scikit-Learn code can be scaled using DaskML with minimal modifications.

- Hyperparameter Search: DaskML's HyperbandSearchCV and GridSearchCV enable parallelized hyperparameter tuning. These tools distribute the search across the cluster, evaluating multiple hyperparameter combinations simultaneously.

- GPU Support: DaskML can leverage GPU resources for computations, further accelerating the training process.

- Model Persistence: Models trained with DaskML can be easily saved and loaded, facilitating deployment in production environments.

- Monitoring and Diagnostics: DaskML benefits from Dask's monitoring tools, allowing users to visualize the computation and diagnose performance bottlenecks.

DaskML represents a significant advancement in the field of scalable machine learning. By integrating the parallel computing power of Dask with machine learning workflows, it opens up new possibilities for handling large-scale data and complex computations. Whether it's preprocessing large datasets, training deep learning models, or performing extensive hyperparameter tuning, DaskML offers a flexible and efficient solution.

Machine Learning Workloads with DaskML

Machine learning workloads refer to the computational tasks involved in training, evaluating, and deploying machine learning models. These workloads can be quite intensive, especially when dealing with large datasets or complex algorithms. Managing these workloads efficiently is crucial for reducing training time, optimizing resource utilization, and ensuring the scalability of machine learning applications.

Managing Machine Learning Workloads with DaskML

The given below is a sample program that demonstrates how to manage machine learning workloads using DaskML:

```
from dask_ml.datasets import make_classification
from dask_ml.model_selection import train_test_split
from dask_ml.linear_model import LogisticRegression
from dask_ml.model_selection import HyperbandSearchCV
from sklearn.metrics import accuracy_score
import dask

# Generate a large dataset
X, y = make_classification(n_samples=1000000, chunks=10000)
X_train, X_test, y_train, y_test = train_test_split(X, y)

# Create a logistic regression model
model = LogisticRegression()
```

```python
# Define hyperparameter search space
param_space = {'C': [0.001, 0.01, 0.1, 1, 10]}

# Use Hyperband for hyperparameter tuning
search = HyperbandSearchCV(model, param_space)
search.fit(X_train, y_train)

# Get the best model
best_model = search.best_estimator_

# Evaluate the model
y_pred = best_model.predict(X_test)
accuracy = accuracy_score(y_test, y_pred)
print("Accuracy:", accuracy)
```

In the above sample program:

- The data is generated and split into training and testing sets.
- A logistic regression model is trained using DaskML.
- HyperbandSearchCV is used to perform hyperparameter tuning in parallel.
- The model's accuracy is evaluated on the test set.

DaskML provides a powerful set of tools to handle these workloads efficiently, enabling scalable and parallelized machine learning. By integrating DaskML into the machine learning pipeline, data scientists and engineers can significantly reduce the time and resources required to train and deploy models, making it an essential tool for large-scale machine learning applications.

Managing Regression Model using DaskML

Managing a regression model using DaskML follows a similar process to classification, but with a focus on predicting continuous values rather than discrete classes. Following is a step-wise walkthrough to managing a regression model using DaskML:

Import Libraries

First, you'll need to import the necessary libraries for working with DaskML and regression models.

```
from dask_ml.datasets import make_regression
from dask_ml.model_selection import train_test_split
from dask_ml.linear_model import LinearRegression
from sklearn.metrics import mean_squared_error
import dask
```

Generate and Split Data

You can create a synthetic regression dataset using the make_regression function and then split it into training and testing sets.

```
X, y = make_regression(n_samples=1000000, n_features=20, chunks=10000)
X_train, X_test, y_train, y_test = train_test_split(X, y)
```

Create and Train the Model

Next, you'll create a linear regression model using DaskML's LinearRegression class and train it on the training data.

```
model = LinearRegression()
model.fit(X_train, y_train)
```

Make Predictions

Once the model is trained, you can use it to make predictions on the test data.

```
y_pred = model.predict(X_test)
```

Evaluate the Model

You can evaluate the performance of the regression model using metrics like Mean Squared Error (MSE).

```
mse = mean_squared_error(y_test, y_pred)
```

```
print("Mean Squared Error:", mse)
```

This sample program demonstrates key steps include generating and splitting the data, creating and training the linear regression model, making predictions, and evaluating the model's performance using the mean squared error. These steps provide a comprehensive workflow for managing regression models with DaskML.

Managing Classification Model

Managing a classification model using DaskML is similar to managing a regression model, but with a focus on predicting discrete classes. Following is a step-wise walkthrough to managing a classification model using DaskML:

Import Libraries

First, you'll need to import the necessary libraries for working with DaskML and classification models.

```
from dask_ml.datasets import make_classification
from dask_ml.model_selection import train_test_split
from dask_ml.linear_model import LogisticRegression
from sklearn.metrics import accuracy_score
import dask
```

Generate and Split Data

You can create a synthetic classification dataset using the make_classification function and then split it into training and testing sets.

```
X, y = make_classification(n_samples=1000000, n_features=20, chunks=10000)
X_train, X_test, y_train, y_test = train_test_split(X, y)
```

Create and Train the Model

Next, you'll create a logistic regression model using DaskML's LogisticRegression class and train it on the training data.

```
model = LogisticRegression()
model.fit(X_train, y_train)
```

Make Predictions

Once the model is trained, you can use it to make predictions on the test data.

```
y_pred = model.predict(X_test)
```

Evaluate the Model

You can evaluate the performance of the classification model using metrics like accuracy.

```
accuracy = accuracy_score(y_test, y_pred)
print("Accuracy:", accuracy)
```

This sample program demonstrates key steps include generating and splitting the data, creating and training the logistic regression model, making predictions, and evaluating the model's performance using accuracy. The main difference from the regression example is the use of a logistic regression model and the make_classification function to generate a classification dataset. Additionally, the evaluation metric is accuracy, which is suitable for classification tasks.

DaskML Key Functions

When working with DaskML, there are several essential functions and classes that you'll commonly use. The given below is a quick overview of some of the key components:

Data Preparation and Preprocessing

- dask_ml.datasets.make_classification: Generates a synthetic classification dataset.

- dask_ml.preprocessing.StandardScaler: Standardizes features by removing the mean and scaling to unit variance.

- dask_ml.model_selection.train_test_split: Splits arrays or matrices into random train and test subsets.

Model Training

- dask_ml.linear_model.LogisticRegression: Logistic regression classifier.

- dask_ml.linear_model.LinearRegression: Linear regression model.

- dask_ml.cluster.KMeans: K-Means clustering.

- dask_ml.ensemble.GradientBoostingClassifier: Gradient Boosting classifier.

Hyperparameter Tuning

- dask_ml.model_selection.GridSearchCV: Exhaustive search over a specified parameter grid.

- dask_ml.model_selection.RandomizedSearchCV: Randomized search over a parameter grid.

Model Evaluation

- dask_ml.metrics.accuracy_score: Accuracy classification score.

- dask_ml.metrics.mean_squared_error: Mean squared error regression loss.

Summary

In this chapter, we embarked on an in-depth journey into the world of DaskML, a specialized library engineered to bring parallel computing to machine learning in Python. The chapter kicked off by dissecting the machine learning pipeline through the lens of computational requirements. It underscored the computational bottlenecks often encountered in machine learning and established the critical need for parallel and distributed computing solutions. DaskML emerged as a robust solution to these challenges, offering a suite of scalable machine learning algorithms adept at managing large-scale data and intricate calculations.

The heart of the chapter was a hands-on walkthrough filled with real-world examples and thorough explanations on leveraging DaskML for diverse machine learning workloads. We explored both regression and classification models, dissecting the nuances in handling these distinct types of predictive algorithms. The chapter provided a deep dive into key functionalities and classes, encompassing everything from data wrangling and preprocessing to model training, hyperparameter optimization, and performance evaluation. These features facilitate the smooth integration of Dask's parallel computing prowess into conventional machine learning pipelines.

To cap it off, we presented specific coding examples that showcased the application of DaskML in tasks like data scaling, model training, and performance assessment. These case studies exemplified the versatility, power, and adaptability of DaskML in tackling real-world machine learning challenges. This chapter armed you with the knowledge and tools to incorporate parallel computing, boosting both efficiency and scalability.

Thank You

Index

B
Batch Processing 46, 48, 49, 115
Best Practices 114, 130

C
Computational Model 14
Custom Algorithms 79

D
Dask Arrays 13, 19, 20, 56, 86, 130, 138
Dask Bags 13, 26, 27, 56
Dask Collection 13
Dask Dashboard 33, 36, 40, 56, 115
Dask DataFrames 7, 13, 14, 23, 26, 49, 56, 94, 96, 97, 99, 100
Dask Delayed 14, 29, 30, 31, 56
Dask Futures 31, 33, 56
DaskML 45, 146, 147, 148, 149, 150, 151, 152, 153
Data Loading 130
Data Locality 66, 69, 130
Data Partitioning 38, 48, 51, 123
Data Preparation 113, 152
Deep Learning 123, 137
Distributed Cluster 62, 77
Distributed Training 120, 122, 124, 126, 127, 147
Dynamic Scheduling 67, 70

E
Error Handling 40, 49, 52, 115

F
Fault Tolerance 73, 131
Feature Extraction 111, 112

G
Google JAX 141, 143
GPU Computing 135, 136, 137
GPU-Accelerated Computing 137
Group Operations 96

H
Hyperparameter Tuning 109, 114, 115, 128, 129, 131, 140, 146, 147, 153

J
Joblib 81, 82, 83, 84, 92
Joint Operations 97

M
Managing Classification 151
Managing Regression 149
Memory Management 38, 137
Model Evaluation 107, 128, 140, 146, 153
Model Selection 105
Model Training 113, 115, 123, 140, 145, 152

N
Numba 15, 84, 85, 86, 87, 92, 116, 131, 136
Numpy 99

P
Pandas 4, 5, 6, 7, 10, 11, 12, 13, 15, 16, 21, 24, 25, 26, 87, 93, 94, 95, 96, 97, 98, 99, 100, 116, 139, 140
Parallelizing 82, 102, 103, 123
Performance Profiling 37, 116
Prefetching 66, 68
Preprocessing 111, 112, 130, 140, 145, 147, 152
PyTorch 118, 119, 120, 121, 122, 123, 124, 125, 126, 128, 129, 130, 132, 137

R
RAPIDS 136, 139, 140, 143
Resource Management 115

S
Scaling Dask Clusters 74
Scikit-Learn 4, 5, 7, 99, 104, 110, 114, 115, 116, 117, 129, 139, 140, 147

T

Task Fusion...67, 72, 132
Task Graphs..10, 14, 55
Task Scheduling..11, 65, 66

X

Xarray..89, 90, 91, 92, 116

Epilogue

As we reach the conclusion of "Parallel Python with Dask," it's time to reflect on the transformative journey we've undertaken. We embarked on this exploration with a fundamental understanding of Python and a desire to delve into the world of parallel computing. What we've discovered is a powerful and flexible tool in Dask that has opened new horizons in data processing, machine learning, and scalability.

The chapters of this book have guided us through the intricate landscape of parallel computing, from the basic concepts of CPU and GPU computing to the advanced techniques of distributed systems and fault tolerance. We've learned how to integrate Dask with popular libraries like Pandas, Scikit-Learn, PyTorch, and more, allowing us to harness the power of parallelism in familiar environments. One of the key takeaways from this book is the realization that parallel computing is not an esoteric field reserved for specialists. With Dask, parallel computing is accessible to anyone with a basic understanding of Python. The practical examples and step-by-step instructions provided throughout the book have demystified complex concepts, making them approachable and applicable in real-world scenarios.

We've also delved into the optimization strategies and best practices that are essential for building robust and efficient parallel applications. These insights equip us with the knowledge to not only implement parallel computing but to do so in a way that maximizes performance and resource utilization. The integration of Dask with various machine learning frameworks has shown us the potential of parallel computing in the rapidly evolving field of artificial intelligence. The ability to train and evaluate models in parallel, perform hyperparameter tuning, and manage large-scale data processing tasks has significant implications for the future of machine learning and data science.

As we close this book, it's important to recognize that the journey doesn't end here. The field of parallel computing is dynamic and constantly evolving. New tools, techniques, and frameworks are being developed, and the applications of parallel computing continue to expand. The knowledge and skills acquired through this book provide a strong foundation, but there is always more to learn and explore.

"Parallel Python with Dask" has equipped us with the tools to transform the way we approach programming and data processing. We've learned to think in parallel, to see opportunities for optimization, and to approach problems with scalability in mind. These are not just technical skills; they are a mindset that can be applied across various domains and industries.

In a world where data is at the core of decision-making, innovation, and progress, the ability to process it efficiently is a valuable asset. Whether you are a developer, data scientist, researcher, or enthusiast, the knowledge gained from this book empowers you to contribute to this exciting field. The journey through "Parallel Python with Dask" has been both challenging and rewarding. It has expanded our understanding, sharpened our skills, and ignited our curiosity. As we turn the final page, we do so with a sense of accomplishment and a readiness to apply what we've learned. The world of parallel computing awaits, and we are now equipped to explore it with confidence and creativity.

Made in the USA
Monee, IL
26 December 2025

40284027R00096